BECOMING

Choosing Grace

BECOMING

Choosing Grace

J. E. Mayhew

Cover: Jamie Mayhew
Cover Photo: King County Jail

J. E. Mayhew
2019

First Printing: 2019
ISBN 978-1-7334093-0-8

J. E. Mayhew
TX, USA
becomingchoosinggrace@gmail.com

To CHOOSE
is to deliberately own, accept, receive, and sustain
as an act of will
with purpose, committed to action.

GRACE is the enabling and ennobling power of the atonement of Jesus Christ. Through the Grace of Jesus Christ, I can be cleansed of my sins and transgressions, and I will be resurrected, uniting my spirit with my body, never to be separated again. Through Grace, I am enabled in my righteous pursuits and desires to do and BECOME what would have otherwise been impossible.

I am not my impulses or desires
I am not my circumstances
I am not my weaknesses
I am not my struggles
I am not my body
I am not defined

I choose
I act

I am becoming!

Contents

Preface

Throughout my life, I have made many mistakes and gained unique growth opportunities. While many of these experiences have taught me valuable lessons, some were difficult to overcome. Most of these lessons could have been learned through the knowledge and experiences of others.

Drug addiction, dropping out of school, trouble with the law, and homelessness are among the struggles discussed. In this book I share my experiences, with some of the lessons and insights I have gained along the way.

While some memories fade with time, I have tried to remain true to the times, events, and impressions of my experiences. Looking back, in some instances, it is difficult to definitively differentiate. It is my desire to address the thoughts and growth experiences of my life. Often the lessons were not learned until long after the event occurred.

I hope to convey these thoughts and experiences in a way that others may benefit, without experiencing the pain. I hope to inspire empathy for those who struggle and may otherwise be difficult to love. I hope to provide context for some self-inflicted suffering and to dissuade others from making similar mistakes.

I am not a writer, and I hope you will forgive my weakness. I hope you will search for meaning and intent in my words. I hope to inspire hope and a desire for good in your life. I hope you find value in this book.

J. E. Mayhew

Introduction

Everyone experiences trials. We all suffer, though some of our suffering is not discernible through simple observation.

Many of life's most valuable lessons may be learned from others. Compassion and consequence are two of life's great teachers. They may be consulted when we seek to learn from our experience with others, if we allow ourselves the opportunity.

Are you willing to take a hypothetical journey with me? To take a moment and imagine your life as another? To assume their trials, their wants, their desires, their confusion, and their pain? Not from your perspective but from theirs?

Let's begin.

***

Who are you?

Where do your troubles nucleate?

Are you socially awkward due to inexperience and a poor perception of the thoughts, feelings, and intentions of others?

Is your home broken?

Are your parents divorced or otherwise in conflict with each other and therefore under or overcompensating their behavior toward you because of their own insecurities or frustrations?

Have your parents abandoned you through death, choice, circumstance, or neglect, leaving you a product of your environment?

Are you the victim of mental, physical, or sexual abuse?

Has your concept of acceptable wholesome human interactions been damaged or destroyed?

Are you at odds with society's expectations, unable or unwilling to discern and adapt to its demands?

Do you experience same-gender attraction contrary to your standard of acceptance or the standards of others?

Do you otherwise struggle with your own self-worth or that defined for you?

Are you addicted to drugs, pornography, or other harmful stimuli?

Are you depressed, insecure, or paranoid?

Are you experiencing compulsive behavior or another mental disorder that you feel powerless to control?

Are you "broken"?

You own your faults and assimilate them into your character and your perception of yourself. Your behavior is modified by this perception and is reflected in your interactions with others. You find every excuse to abandon expectation, regulation, and authority—in the woods, at the park, at a friend's house, on a bus, or on a train.

You yearn to distract yourself. Mischievousness and folly naturally accompany your undisciplined exploration but only lead you to greater dangers.

Social interactions are filled with guilt, awkwardness, confusion, and an absence of purpose and consistently provide an awareness of your broken nature as you attempt to define normal.

The innate insecurities of adolescence and self-discovery are magnified and compounded in you. Your peers perceive weakness and a lack of self-worth through your silence, poor hygiene, awkwardness, sadness, anger, or fear.

In comparing themselves to you, they attempt to establish a quality or correctness to their lives or situations, masking their own weakness. For some, widening this divide brings vain satisfaction as they attempt to suffocate their insecurities by feeding yours. They seek to crush you through ridicule, violence, social or emotional deprivation, or worse. You are abandoned.

Are you comfortable enough with yourself and your desires for life to withstand these assaults and attempt to find healthy relationships with those who are socially and emotionally mature enough to refrain from engaging in these activities?

Do you know what a healthy relationship looks like or feels like?

Do you know how to reciprocate in such a relationship and be positive and contributing?

No, you don't.

You put up walls. These walls manifest themselves as anger, humor, sarcasm, cynicism, apathy, or pathetic silence in an attempt to hide your "broken parts."

You find other "broken" people who reject empathy primarily because they perceive it as a weakness in their emotional immaturity. They lack the experience to know how to respond to empathy in socially acceptable ways. You, however, reject empathy and joyful expectation because of the accompanying pain and disappointment of your personal narrative. You have forfeited love and hope. You are withdrawn.

With healthy social and emotional growth abandoned, you seek to fill these basic human needs with corrosive counterfeits. Rebellion, with its deceptive sense of autonomy, leads you down forbidden paths of thrill-seeking, greed, addiction, sexual promiscuity, and criminal activity.

Self-gratification successfully masquerades as purpose, fulfillment, and happiness because you have either forgotten or never learned otherwise. You become a parasite, ever consuming, never satisfied. Addiction is your hope in your hopelessness as your pursuit and purpose yield to these primal desires.

Engulfed in self-loathing you contemplate suicide as your thoughts and memories mock your pain. You are alone, so very alone.

No one can see you.

No one can hear you.

No one can care about you.

This reality will continue as long as you live inside your perception of yourself.

No one will see, hear, or love you until you remove your carapace of pain, indulgence, and self-loathing and submit yourself to the truth all feel in those quiet moments of release and acceptance.

***

Stepping into the life of another, without judgment, prejudice, or expectation, can unlock a portion of our heart that defies rational thought. We can enter a realm of paradox and find strength empowered by vulnerability, hope defying despair, and love extinguishing fear. We can find Grace. We can choose, regardless of circumstance or expectation.

Empathy yields to Apathy
as idle pleasures hypnotize.

Twisted truth and controversy,
narcissism justifies.

Apathy to Enmity,
amid the humble cries—

Their victory, a tragedy
united by dividing ties.

Compassion dies.

PART I – CHOOSING

Wake-Up Call

"Hey, Mayhew! Today is your 18th birthday, isn't it? I should arrest you just because I can."

Defeated, I let out a sigh and looked up to find a police officer glaring back at me from the front seat of his car, with a smirk on his face. I looked around at the empty park. Flintstone Freeway, so aptly named because of the prehistoric looking concrete car that adorns the garden by the roadside.

The park is well manicured with winding paths, picnic tables, public bathrooms, and a dock for fishing and temporary boat access. I wandered down here to catch a bus, but I was moving a bit slow as I wasn't feeling particularly festive.

The officer, unflinching, waited for me to slide down off the picnic table and onto the bench. I was in violation of a city ordinance that prohibits sitting on top of picnic tables. Once my hind quarters were firmly placed on the bench, he drove on, biding his time until we met again.

For years, I had been living a life of rebellion, frivolity, and excess, wasting my days and my strength for that which could not satisfy. The hole in my soul continued to erode from the corrosive material with which I attempted to fill it. I had little respect for myself and likewise showed little respect to others. I had all but given up on life and myself.

Void of any real hope for the future, I was just waiting to die. My anger, depression, and rebellion had coalesced into a defiant cocoon of despair. I was hopeless, yet I was desensitized to its defeating influence. It was my normal.

Childhood

My childhood was much like many other kids' who grew up in rural suburbia. We lived in a secluded neighborhood where many empty lots provided an extensive natural playground. I would spend much of my time outside, exploring and testing the limits of my imagination.

Secretly, I imagined myself as a Native American prior to "modernization." I was in love with the idea of living off the land. I treasured the thought that I could decipher the purpose of creation and use it, in its raw beauty, to build a life. The trees for shelter, art, and fire. Rich red silt or clay stone for pigments and pottery. Herbs for nutrition and medicine. I wanted to be strong and self-sufficient. I wanted to be left alone.

As a child in a military family, we were stationed on an island in western Washington. I grew accustomed to and loved the ocean, mountains, trees, rain, wildlife, and all four seasons. From our backyard I could see majestic mountains, a tree covered island, a local bay, and the water in-between. For a time, we were visited by a family of bald eagles who made their perch in a tree down the street.

Often, I found myself preferring seclusion and solitude. These moments of isolation would lend themselves to reflection, introspection, and imagination. These pastimes have remained with me, and I find they can be a good benchmark if I track their progress through time.

From a very early age, I wanted to be wise. I distinctly remember blowing the seeds off dandelions, wishing to be the strongest man in the world, until one day I realized that physical strength fades with time. My desires turned to wisdom. Something I felt I could take with me.

Within a year or two, at the age of nine, our family was uprooted from our home to relocate to a suburb of London, England. This adventure introduced me to a new world of experience and opportunity. Almost overnight I found myself in another country, in a military housing neighborhood full of children from multiple NATO affiliated countries.

British Boy Scouts and traveling around Europe with my family opened my eyes to some beauties and experiences I had not previously considered. I loved the opportunity to live in an area with an extensive documented history, an experience that was difficult to grasp in Washington. We had, however, been blessed with a rich Native American history, though I was too young at the time to appreciate it.

This new life in England was not without its challenges. I navigated through a new social structure and attempted to understand and conform to the expectations of others. I struggled to balance difficulties at home with neighborhood relationships, life at school, and a new setting at church. These confusing situations were only compounded by the disruptive, confusing circumstances of preadolescence.

Social interactions were often strained. I found myself the object of ridicule. Silence, submission, and sarcasm dominated my response structure.

England is where I was first introduced to the recreational use of tobacco, alcohol, and drugs in young adults. I was confronted with many ironies that conflicted with the purist perspective I grew accustomed to in my orthodox "Mormon" upbringing. Good people doing "bad" things didn't seem to fit the narrative in my mind.

Physical and emotional abuse compounded within as I rarely took any discernible steps to combat them, only building walls and suppressing response. When I did take steps, it was to fight.

Slowly, I began to retreat as I rarely felt as though I "fit in." It was easier to return to my seclusion, though now I would occasionally share it with a friend. We found respite in a local forest or an old abandoned house.

My retreat and rebellion intensified. I could not be contained. I would wander farther and farther from home.

I was conflicted by the hypocrisy of imperfect people who seemingly expected perfection (or so I told myself). I'm not exactly sure what sparked this thought. Likely, it was the combination of what I was taught, what I thought, how I was treated, and my own personal temptations.

I believed that there was an elusive truth, perspective, or understanding that could explain the conflict, yet I could not find it or understand it, if I had found it.

Religion, with its niceties, metaphors, and generalities, did not seem to sink in with me, at least not how I thought it was intended to. I maintained my belief in God, though I don't think I believed He played an active role in my life.

I was in trouble—a lot. I didn't know how or why I should change. I decided that I could "figure it out" for myself. My troubled, exhausted mind believed that if I gave into my temptations and thoughts, I could more fully understand them.

How could I have a firm faith in God and the existence of truth and have so many temptations and struggles?

Why was I bad?

What made me bad?

Why did people neglect or reject the truth?

I decided I would discover the answers to these questions so I could help myself and, presumptuously, others. In hindsight, this childish, ridiculous, and extremely arrogant sentiment does not approach rational thought, though such was the rationale of a young boy's mind. My perspective molded my reality and, as irrational as it was, I believed it, therefore it was possible.

By the age of 12, I had all but given up on counsel as I had decided "I could figure it out on my own." I don't think I understood why my life came with so many spiritual difficulties, and I can't compare the inner workings of my young mind to anyone else.

I questioned—a lot.

As the earth's horizon
dominates my heavenly sphere,
Confusion
blankets my every breath.
The devil's reign
begins again,
as another night comes.

If you could join me
in my world,
all that you would see—
everything,
is distant,
gone forever.
Alone are you and me.

Firmly fixed around my neck,
another cursed noose.
If only I could make it end,
the world and I
would call a truce.

But alone am I—
Paranoid.
Darkness is my fight.
A ray of hope to save my peace,
I find myself,
and pray my grief deceased.

You bastards!
You betrayed me,
appearing so pure and clean.
Corruption is for the weak.
Strong am I,
and strong I will always be.

Adolescence

My time in England brought me closer to conflict. The Irish Republican Army (IRA) continued to protest British involvement in Northern Ireland, the Gulf War disrupted daily life, and the Berlin wall came crashing down during our stay overseas.

The Gulf War was particularly disruptive. We would stay up late watching the events unfold in near real-time, as many of the operations were conducted at night. I attended school on a NATO base where heightened security was a bit traumatic. Our bus was searched, inside and out, every day before entering the base. Bomb-sniffing dogs outside and humorless marines inside.

In the seventh grade, my middle school was condemned due to its proximity to a large communications satellite. The seventh- and eighth-graders were moved into the high school nearby. While I understood this was for our safety, the bomb threats and emergency drills were less than conducive to a rich learning environment.

***

About my 13th birthday, we moved back to the states. This time we landed on the east coast, on an island in Rhode Island.

Arriving back in the states had its own set of peculiarities to deal with. Entering teenage years while having to try and make new friends provided a lot of opportunity for conflict and discovery.

Living in a young military community, it was easy for a teenager to get alcohol. Everything from traditional beer to Thunder Horse to blackberry brandy to Sambuca liquor, which tasted like black licorice.

Adrenaline and addiction excited my immediate senses and drowned my character and will. The more I welcomed and allowed external stimuli to molest my mind and my body, the more I became a slave to their enticing influence.

Girls began to occupy my thoughts more frequently, though I was unsure of how to interact with them. One young lady offered to "educate" me when she discovered I had not been intimate with a woman before. Her parents were unapologetic about their sexuality and pornography.

My first exposure to pornography had begun in the woods of England, a few years prior, when I stumbled upon a magazine. Since that time, its influence over me had only grown.

Participating in any selfish sexual indulgence masquerades as connection, though it is purely parasitic. It creates a false sense of belonging, ever consuming, never replenishing. I fed only to end hungrier than when I started.

I allowed myself to be acted upon by my emotions, my selfish desires, and the unhealthy stimuli I invited. Thievery fueled my lifestyle. Friendship can be bought, so long as you're the one buying. When you have money for cigarettes, drugs, alcohol, or even just gas money, you can find someone who will let you tag along.

***

In ninth grade, I began participating in Army ROTC at a neighboring high school. I found structure and an opportunity to take my mind off of some of my difficulties. I felt like I was participating in something meaningful. I enjoyed the survival training; it brought me back to feelings I had when I was younger.

We marched in the 1993 St. Patrick's Day parade, which traversed the city of Newport, landing us back at the Newport High School. That was the day the "Storm of the Century" hit New England.

There was something wrong with the phone communications, and I was unable to contact my dad for a ride home. I wasn't the only one.

We all watched outside as the snow began to pile up. It was whiteout conditions, and we were sure our parents wouldn't be able to come get us, even if we could contact them. So we decided to walk.

We began navigating our way through downtown Newport. The snowbanks were piling high, and some cars needed help getting out. We were stopped briefly by a salty old veteran who decided to give us a little lesson in military behavior, since we were still dressed in our BDUs.

He stopped us in our tracks and insisted that we present ourselves in true military fashion. He even drilled us a little. We didn't argue. He was a large man and slightly inebriated, so we were a little unsure of him. We thought it best to let him do whatever he was doing and then be on our way.

We found ourselves very cold and wet. We took shelter in an upscale hotel, where we were able to use the laundry room and put some of our outerwear in the dryer.

We set out again, heading for home. We left part of our party in the hotel as they planned to wait out the storm.

For a time, I was free. Amidst the chaos of the snow and the storm, we were primarily alone. Alone and unregulated, I was able to do for myself, to act, to move, to survive as we trekked through the snow.

While at the time this experience may not have seemed extraordinary, I believe it taught me a certain level of perseverance and resilience. In the solitude of those streets, I was focused yet lighthearted. I was determined yet at peace. The tranquil beauty of the snow was sublime as it softened the landscape, drifting against the hard lines of Newport's concrete jungle.

Eventually, we made it to a friend's house, where we could wait to contact our parents and get a ride home.

Spiritual War

During the summer of my 15th birthday, we returned to the town of my nativity. My willful descent was in full swing. Within the first year, I dropped out of high school and fully gave myself over to selfishness, criminality, and addiction. I forsook choice and accountability for my desires, emotions, and appetites. My hope resided in the next experience, the next stimuli, rarely projecting far into the future.

I was lost.

Misery, pain, addiction, lasciviousness, and indulgence condescendingly sated my body's parasitic desires with the brutal intention of emaciating and ultimately destroying my soul. I deprived myself of the mental, emotional, social, and spiritual growth that is essential during those crucial adolescent years.

For many years I allowed my desires and impulses to feed off my soul. Property and possession were no barriers for me. I entered forbidden places, took things that belonged to others, and allowed violence to consume me in the moment.

While I did not often seek it out, at times I found myself caught in altercations, responding impulsively to interference or following paths that ultimately led to violence.

I was destructive – and it almost destroyed me.

My addiction to physical and emotional stimuli robbed me of an accurate sense of reality, including an understanding of love, relationships, and how I fit into the world around me. That deprivation only encouraged a deeper dive into the abyss.

Sin, and the associated despair that accompanies honest, though short-sighted, reflection, produced a profound loneliness that challenged my very existence. Much of my consciously destructive behavior can be attributed to my vain attempts to mask the deeper more enduring spiritual damage caused by my thoughts, actions and ultimately my perspective of myself and those around me. Consolation in my "natural self" only aggravated the wound and perpetuated the destructive cycle.

Many of my social interactions involved violence, tobacco, alcohol, drugs, or women. Since being exposed to pornography at a young age, and my descent into selfishness and appetite, I could not define a healthy, intimate, relationship, let alone participate in one. My behavior and thoughts were selfish and consuming, though in my heart I know I yearned for something more.

At times, I would drink myself into a deep intoxicating despair that seemingly bordered on normality. Life and reality would fade from reasonable perception, and in my stupor my life wouldn't seem so bad. It almost felt like "this is the way it is supposed to be." It was my new normal. At least until the sickness set in and I found myself embodying weakness.

I lived a transient lifestyle. I wandered from house to house, party to party, and hole to hole, ever consuming never fulfilled. There rarely seemed to be a shortage of unmonitored places to go. On a couple of occasions, friends' parents gave them an old rundown single-wide mobile home to live in. These turned into magnets for the addicted and irresponsible.

My small band of friends became night dwellers. Afraid of the light, we masked our deeds in darkness. We were near boundless in our wanderings. All experiences, feelings, and possessions were ours for the taking if we could but muster the compulsion.

I avoided home as much as possible, though I found solace at my friend's house. His family seemed to have accepted me as-is. If they judged me, it didn't show.

I went where I wanted and did what I wanted. I lived what I believed was freedom, yet life held little joy. Death was no threat and at times a welcomed guest. If this was the best life had to offer, why was it so burdensome and exhausting?

My lifestyle was unsustainable. There was no satisfaction so I continued to bury myself deeper. Ultimately, I began experimenting with mind-altering, hallucinogenic drugs that took me "outside of myself."

Tripping on LSD is not something you do so much as it is something that happens to you. I had several experiences with LSD, many of which ended without incident. Others left an impact long after the initial trip wore off.

***

One summer a buddy of mine and I, along with another young fellow, took a bus down to Seattle to attend a festival the next day. We had very little money and no prospects other than attending Hempfest.

After taking a bus, a ferry, then another bus, we found ourselves at Myrtle Edwards Park. It was already after dark when we came across a school bus converted into a hippie's dream. In front of the bus was a table providing soup, and a group in a circle providing entertainment. We all played hackysack and chatted the night away.

Our party slowly dwindled and we needed to find lodging of our own. Until this point we had given it little thought. We wandered around looking for a suitable location, finally deciding to sleep on the side of a hill, across the street from a few shops and the water.

The next morning we made our way back to Myrtle Edwards Park to participate in the festivities. The park was teeming with people, and there was no shortage of marijuana. In fact, there was an older gentleman, posted up at a picnic table, filling pipes from a cooler of ganja at his side.

A stage occupied one side of a field where presentations were made touting the benefits of marijuana. One representative from the university even started a chainsaw with hemp oil.

While in the park, we met with an older free-loving gentleman and his companion. They offered us LSD in exchange for about $20. We had never experienced LSD before, so we weren't sure what to expect. After paying him, he pulled out a vial and poured a strange liquid into our hands. It pooled in my palm and produced an iridescent sheen.

Afraid of spilling it, we quickly lapped it up. From my later experience with the drug and its administration, I estimate this may have been a massive overdose. Typically, LSD is given in "hits" comprised of small dipped pieces of paper, or another vehicle used to administer the drug in small doses.

The effects were severe. As they intensified, only a few fragments of the remaining hours can be accounted for. I was able to call my dad and ask him to travel the two-plus hours (one-way) to come and get us.

Then we ordered two hamburgers at McDonalds and waited for our ride.

Staring at the plant foliage at the edge of the restaurant, my mind was swept away into oblivion. I do not recall exactly how we got home, though I maintain a vague recollection of being interrogated by my father.

***

LSD or "acid" was always welcome whenever I could get it. I would not be dissuaded, whether by overdose, bad acid, or simply by life catching up with me. I had a severe reaction to one trip that left its mark long after the affects wore off.

After being dropped off the evening of my reaction, I went straight to sleep. Whether the next day or the day after, when I left my room it was dark outside, though not so late that everyone was sleeping. I walked into the den where other family members were watching TV. The den was in the corner of the house, with the TV in the corner, flanked by two large windows. Couches sat opposite each window.

With curtains open and the dark ocean view outside, the windows acted as near perfect reflectors of the lights within, though shadowed by the darkness without. As I looked up, from the window on the left, I saw the headlights of a large dump truck coming directly at me.

My mind was hit by that truck and my body responded accordingly. I immediately convulsed and landed on the couch to my right. Getting myself up, I moved back to bed.

For several months to follow, it was difficult to focus my thoughts, and I developed a rather distinct stutter when I spoke. Still, I had not, as of yet, learned my lesson.

When illegal drugs could not be found, other over-the-counter medications were sufficient substitutes. A bottle of a certain cold medicine was enough to get two people high, with significant effects.

With this lifestyle I found myself in and out of court, the drunk tank, and house arrest. Up to this point I had somehow managed to avoid juvenile hall, though I was quickly about to age out.

In spite of my reckless, aimless, destructive behavior, I was able to find companionship. These relationships were often susceptible to deceit, selfishness, and lasciviousness. Relationships were primarily consumptive, regardless of how much we claimed connection. We'd feed off of each other's appetites and insecurities.

I wanted to love and be loved, but I had no idea what that looked like nor what to do with it if I found it. A couple of times I believe I got close, but my need and addiction suffocated it before I had a chance.

Powers and Passions
carry a deafening tone.
Milk them for their pleasure;
in the end you're left alone.

You have lost your connection
to the only peace in life.
You feel proud pain
as day turns into night.

Charisma and Charm
have a flattering effect,
yet dim throughout the years,
leaving you cold and heartless.
Who's there to kiss your tears?

Wither away,
letting your petals fall.
Death comes to you quickly.
Now say goodbye
to all that could have been.

Adulting

So there I was, sitting in the park on my eighteenth birthday, wondering what to do with my life. I had some experience with manual labor, but I possessed few, if any, marketable skills. High school dropouts were not in high demand, especially not those who were known personally by local law enforcement, and not in a good way.

I did a lot of odd jobs and piece work. I also spent a short time working on a chicken farm one summer. However, most of my work experience came while performing community service, both at court order and to pay fines I was otherwise unable to pay.

I was particularly fond of my work for the county road crew. I worked closely with the mechanic, who taught me the value of work and how to care for things to make them last. He showed me respect and trust, and I am grateful to this day for his example.

I helped him maintain the shop and vehicles. I was able to accompany the crews a few times to sealcoat roads, repair damaged asphalt, and clean up tree debris. I don't remember how many times I went to work for him, though it lasted for a few seasons.

Unfortunately, my lifestyle got the better of me and I didn't show up for work, so he fired me. That may have been one of the greatest lessons he ever taught me.

I had another round of community service coming up, and I needed to find a new place to do it. Apparently, misrepresenting (selling) vitamins as methamphetamine to a police informant is considered an offense. An offense, I found out the hard way, that earned me five days in jail, a hefty fine, and a stack of community service.

On top of that, I had community service from driving without a license. I had driven my buddy's car from the front of the restaurant (bar) to the back of the restaurant (bar). He had a headlight out and the state trooper didn't like that too much.

***

So early one misty morning, I was dropped off outside of the county jail. Slowly, I entered to report for my time. While I had experienced multiple rounds of house arrest, this was the first time I would spend more than a few hours in a jail cell and the first time I would be placed with a population of adults.

Upon entering the building, I was ushered to a processing station where officers received me. They relieved me of all my possessions, then placed me in a large, cold, concrete room.

Once inside, I removed all of my clothing and paraded myself before the guards, ensuring them that I was not smuggling anything into the building. Once satisfied, I received my "uniform," was handed my linens, and then escorted to my cell.

We entered a small cell block on the second level. Approximately twelve cells in all, six above and six below. Each cell had a steel bed with a thin, hard mattress, which felt as if it was covered in duct tape. The sink was about the size of a salad bowl, and the steel toilet wasn't much bigger.

My only consolations were that I had a single room and the doors shut at night. Sleep did not come easy because many of the lights remained lit. The room filled with a hollow eeriness that helped me realize just how alone I was. Sounds were amplified against the backdrop of steel and concrete.

There was only a single shower, open to the main floor except for a simple curtain. I could go five days without a shower. It wasn't the first time and it wouldn't be the last.

My block mates weren't hardened criminals. I took the time and learned to play cribbage. It seemed to be the pastime of choice, and that was what I wanted most—to pass the time.

Our available exercise ended up being a large concrete room with a racquetball. I was told that was my opportunity to play handball, but no one seemed interested. The main attraction, for me, was the fresh air that was wafting in from a grated opening about 15 feet or so up on the side of one wall.

The meals weren't horrible, though they weren't fantastic either, about on par for any cafeteria type. Lunch was usually predictable as it appeared to be some recycled version of "last night's dinner."

I wondered who might come to visit me while in jail. Would anyone?

I did have visitors. My mom came and so did a few friends. It was nice that they spaced it out over the few days I was in there. It helped to get out of my cell.

My five-day stint was not very long, especially compared to the guys who had six-month sentences, the longest term allowed, I think, before they were sent upstate.

Finally, my release time came, but they dawdled and I found myself waiting until almost lunch before I was processed to leave. I admit, I did not handle the wait gracefully.

My mom picked me up. She asked if I was ready to quit smoking since I had already gone five days without. I had little to look forward to in my life, and that was one of the simple pleasures I was not ready to give up. Smoking is hope for the hopeless. No matter how hard or desperate life got, I could always look forward to having a cigarette.

I set up community service at the nursing home my mom was working at. I was able to help out with the maintenance crew, performing basic janitorial and handyman work.

This time my community service actually landed me a job. First washing dishes, then working in the maintenance shop. This was a new experience for me—I had a constant flow of money. This new income helped to fund everything from a spontaneous weekend trip to Las Vegas, to the purchase of a motorcycle, to a more expensive and potent drug addiction.

Methamphetamines became my new "drug of choice" (besides marijuana), with cocaine and LSD added in when I could get them. These types of drugs had been a part of my life before but only intermittently, because I could rarely afford them or find an adequate "sponsor."

My depression and disdain for life took a new turn. Addiction now also manifested itself in adrenaline. The purchase of a 900cc Kawasaki Ninja provided the opportunity for excessive speeds and extremely dangerous acceleration.

I also passed the time repelling and free climbing the cliffs to the north. Large limestone cliffs provided interesting opportunities for large jumps and rapid descents.

One day a friend of mine and I thought it would be fun to sit on a ledge about a third of the way down a 150-foot cliff to smoke a bowl.

I went first. After landing on the ledge, I let out enough rope to allow my friend to come sit down next to me. The ledge was only a couple feet wide and a few inches deep. We sat and talked with a gentleman on the bridge while we smoked. He was kind and a little jealous he couldn't join us.

After our short interlude, we decided it was time to head down. As you might have guessed, that is when we realized one of us would have to unhook from the rope and sit on the ledge while the other repelled down.

My friend decided I should go first. I got into position, swung out, and dropped down several feet. In doing so, I dislodged a rock, about 7 to 8 inches in diameter, at the top, where my rope met the cliff.

I watched this rock fall, as if in slow motion, as it tumbled against the face of the cliff. I positioned myself below my friend as I saw the rock head straight for him. While he gripped the cliff as tightly as possible, I watched in horror as the rock struck him square in the back. He then slowly rolled to one side and let the rock fall.

After asking if he was okay, he assured me he was and proceeded to encourage me to descend the cliff as rapidly as possible. We both made it off the cliff alive, but he was not without a large jagged bloody wound.

To the Pain

The night before my 19th birthday, I returned home late, high on meth. I entered through the garage and noticed that the faring to my ninja, which I had been repairing, was destroyed. After a brief inspection, I noticed a bit of fiberglass on the handgrip and deduced that someone had knocked my bike over and broken it.

I entered the house in a rage and my roommate owned up to the act, though, as I determined, rather smugly. In a fit of vulgarity and aggression, I stormed down the hall while my roommate yelled after me. In response, I slammed my door shut and proceeded to kick it clear of its hinges. Unhinging my door successfully unhinged my roommate, and he ran down the hall, entering my room hell-bent on violence.

Unfortunately for him, he was no match for my drug imbued body, void of pain and fear. Immersed in my depression and despair, there was little I held dear. I grappled his throat and mercilessly assaulted his head and body until he crumpled on the threshold of my room.

I watched him, face down, for what seemed like minutes, though may have only amounted to mere seconds, before he leapt to his feet and ran for his room. Knowing him as I did, I immediately assumed the object of his retreat.

His sword.

Clearing the room, I ran for the kitchen, where I might more readily maneuver. Little did I think that this would be to his advantage and not mine. Staring down the long hall, I could just see into his room before my view was obstructed by the wall of his closet.

Within moments he crashed into his door from the side, then barreled down the hallway with his short sword brandished above his head. I stood motionless next to the refrigerator until just after he entered the kitchen. He swung for my left side as I ducked behind the refrigerator. My left hand connected with his sword hand. Both our hands fell to my side. He immediately returned and cut a large gash on my upper arm.

Blood quickly began to flow down my arm. I am unsure what happened next, but I received multiple scratches and minor lacerations before he was able to take his sword to my chest.

The tip of his sword entered my chest about the third rib up, and about an inch off center to my left. The orientation of the sword prevented it from piercing my rib cage. Whether by mercy, chance, or a lack of experience killing "meth-heads," my roommate allowed me to live another day.

Within seconds, following a brief scuffle, our little dance was interrupted by our landlady who, living beneath us, heard the commotion and quickly came to investigate. Observing me as I was, and likely gravitating to her innate understanding of my character through simple observation, immediately determined I was at fault and evicted me from the premises.

I jumped on my motorcycle, full of drugs, adrenalin, and rage, and rode to a friend's house. We immediately turned around and returned so that I could retrieve some of my most valued possessions: a couple of cartons of smokes in my top dresser drawer.

Before I could gather my things, I was placed in handcuffs and politely escorted to the back of a police car. I was able to observe the dialogue between the officer, my roommate, and our landlady, though I was unable to hear.

Eventually, enough of the truth came out such that I was released and told I could return in the morning, with a police escort, to retrieve the rest of my things.

The hospital visit was less than cordial as I received multiple stitches and a good talking-to from the attending physician. I had long since come down off my high, though I was cracking jokes in an attempt to make the situation seem less than it was.

The doctor was not impressed and felt I should have approached the situation with a bit more respect and sobriety. She was speaking particularly to the cut in my chest.

***

I quickly found another roommate. This time much closer to work.

Life continued as it had. I scrambled, in vain, from one pursuit to another. I allowed my supervisor to be pushed out so I could take his place, giving me the opportunity to feel accomplished, while my boss had the opportunity to pay less. I then hired a friend of mine whose girlfriend was expecting a baby, though I failed to inform my boss of our relationship.

My friend did not work out and my boss told me to fire him. I refused to, so I quit. Shortly afterward my friend quit too.

In the throes of all this, I lost my apartment. My previous roommate had ferrets that trashed the carpet, and I was liable for the damage because he moved out before I did. So, when I got into another place, I was quickly denied and asked to leave because of the negative reference.

I ended up living in a friend's attic for a few weeks. I got a great job mowing lawns for the city parks department, though I failed my pre-employment drug test.

The HR rep was incredibly kind to me. He gave me a few weeks to get clean before asking me to take another test. When the time came, he took me into his office and asked if I was ready to take another test. I assured him that I wasn't, so he gave me the opportunity to resign, which I did.

During this time I continued to follow impulsive behavior, ever grasping for the unattainable. I searched for meaning and purpose in superficiality, rarely recognizing truth and depth when it was before me. If I did recognize it, I didn't know what to do with it.

I found companionship with a young lady who incited feelings that transcended my typical understanding of relationship. These feelings were independent and abiding. I could not will the experience to be, any more than I could will it not to be. I was but an observer and an ungrateful participant as I failed to acknowledge the relationship for what it was and treated it as another object of consumption.

I ignorantly and selfishly starved the opportunity. I attempted to own it and, in my arrogance, I pretended to control it, as if I could decide if or when these feelings would be. In the process, I offended one who, had I had eyes to see, could have taught me to see, to feel, to be, love.

***

All the pieces of my life were falling apart, so I took a friend up on an offer to live with him and his family in Las Vegas. I packed my things onto my motorcycle and proceeded to ride from western Washington to Las Vegas.

Somewhere in central Idaho, I stopped for gas. After a quick rest and refuel, I headed back to the highway. As I entered the on-ramp, seconds away from massive acceleration and velocities up to 110 mph, the stretched chain on my bike slipped, lodged itself, and locked up my back tire, skidding me to a halt. A brief pause and reflection told me how narrowly I had avoided an almost certain catastrophe.

A very kind elderly gentleman gave me and my bike a ride to the shop, where I was first given a chain I couldn't afford. They then swapped it out for a cheaper one, much to my shame and poverty.

Back on the road, I made it into Utah. Just south of the Salt Lake City metro area, where buildings were scarce and fields aplenty, I approached my next obstacle. I saw darkness on the horizon, touching the road in front of me. Everything in the distance became a dark blur and it was difficult to discern distance.

About a mile or two out, I watched a large semi-truck enter the void, only to be consumed. At this point I was certain of the situation—an abrupt and intense storm.

There was a wall of heavy rain in front of me and I was approaching it fast. I entered the storm looking and waiting for the first exit or overpass I could find. Immediately adjacent to my position on the highway was a small corral. I assume this was used to gather range cattle at the end of the season, though it was abandoned at the time.

At the exact moment I was passing the enclosure, a shaft of lightning crashed through the sky, bifurcating above the corral and connecting with multiple metal posts in a brilliant display of light and sound that about shook me from my seat.

This moment of terror gave me a small sense of humility as I witnessed, front row, some of the great powers of nature. I then took shelter at a nearby gas station and waited for the storm to pass.

***

Once in Vegas, I was able to secure a job at an extended stay hotel. This was only made possible because my friend's girlfriend was clean and was willing to help me cheat on my drug test. Unfortunately, the job required manual labor outside in the blistering Vegas summer. Conditions my northern body had not grown accustomed to. That job lasted all of about a day.

After working a job for a temp agency, filling boxes in a warehouse, I got a job filling a punch list for a large apartment complex that was under construction. Positive performance would land me a good job as the complex maintenance guy.

The days were long and extremely hot. I inspected apartments and found my way to the office to sit in the air conditioning while I filled out my paperwork.

Being only a couple of miles from home, I would race home on my motorcycle at lunchtime to be with friends. My trips to and from work were designed for maximum efficiency (speed, lots of speed).

One day while traveling down Nellis Boulevard, between Charleston and Sahara, the semi in front of me tapped his brakes. I was in the middle lane. The speed limit was about 45 mph. I looked to my left and saw a Suburban, so I hit the throttle and jumped in front of it as the braking semi closed off my retreat.

After entering the left lane, I saw, to my horror, two parked cars at about the front bumper of the semi. I didn't even have enough time to swear. I tried.

My bike slid sideways and slammed on the asphalt while my body struck the rear end of a parked car. I somehow ended up on my bare back in the gravelly median. I lay there motionless for a moment, assessing the damage to my body before moving. Hand, shoulder, knee, and back had all taken a hit. My best guess was that my hand and knee both hit the car; my shoulder impacted my helmet as my helmet hit the car; and my bare back received the brunt of the road rash. I looked up through my sunglasses and saw someone in the car mouth from their air-conditioned comfort, "Is he dead?"

The pavement was extremely hot on my bare, assaulted skin. After determining nothing was damaged beyond movement, I peeled myself up off the pavement and began assessing my bike. Faring destroyed, left handlebar dangling, and the left foot peg torn off. Police, ambulance, and tow trucks appeared in no time. My buddy's dad showed up in his van just as the officer asked me if I wanted them to trash my motorcycle.

Determined to repair my bike, I picked it up to deposit it in the back of the van, when I noticed a three-inch hole in the engine block. Defeated, I dropped the bike and turned it over to be retrieved and disposed of.

Coming to Myself

I was at a crossroads in my life. I was not sure what the final catalyst was, but I began to come to myself. I started to step out of my own selfish thoughts and pursuits. The world began to open up before me as I considered the depth and purpose of my existence.

The initial purpose and reasoning for my rebellious experiment began to return, slowly inching its way back into my desire and understanding. God was allowed back into my life. He had been evicted for so long that I had a difficult time hearing His voice.

In spite of my selfish retreat, He was ever-present. He remained throughout my struggles and rebellion. Due to His infinite Grace and love, my path gave me experience and understanding without becoming forever lost. In mercy, the Lord hedged up the way before me that I did not prosper in my pursuits. Ever designed to humble and temper my impulsiveness, Jesus Christ walked with me on my darkest road.

If only I had had eyes to see and ears to hear the Lord's whisperings to me earlier, I might have avoided disaster. To have walked the high road and followed the promptings of the Holy Spirit, I would have been spared much of my deepest heartache and sorrow. Yet, the Lord in His mercy took my rebellion and turned it to my experience and good, helping me better understand evil that I might more readily appreciate love.

It was during this time that I spoke with God for the first time since my withdrawal. I felt confusion and a foreboding over my life.

Late at night, I stepped into a dark open construction site and began to pour out my soul to God. Though my thoughts and speech were muddled and halting, my heart began to yearn as never before. My soul was singing but my words came short.

I was desperate. I felt an urgency in my life, my path, and my pursuits. I knew something had to change, though I was unsure of what or how. I believed in God, though I sought a reassurance to know. I was unfamiliar with how the Lord communicates with His children, and why.

I ignorantly sought a physical audience with the Almighty, unaware of the depth of my spiritual betrayal and my nothingness before God in my current state. In mercy, He hid His face from me, though His Spirit was present throughout our discourse.

He did not leave me comfortless. I felt an assurance in my heart, though I was unsure of how to extrapolate it into action in my life. In desperation, I pled to know. To know Him, His love, and His desires for me in my life.

Looking up at Sunrise Mountain, I received an answer.

I felt to know that I was embarking on a path that required faith in following, and that the Lord would not give me the end from the beginning. There is great value in the discovery.

Perception is reality. To find purpose, I needed to look outside of myself. I needed to see things as they truly were and not as I willed them to be.

***

In desperate need of hope, I first focused on worldly pursuit and progress. Meeting with representatives from Job Corps, we identified a

Job Corps campus in eastern Washington and started to make arrangements for my travel to Spokane.

About October or November, I was on an airplane. I left some of my only true friends in Las Vegas. They had been with me, without reservation and judgment, through some of my more formidable years. They are never forgotten.

From Las Vegas to Curlew, Washington, desert sand to snow-covered hills. Curlew Job Corps was a respite for a few weeks. Nestled in the forests of northeastern Washington, the campus was a peaceful moment surrounded by real people. All of the students I met and interacted with seemed to be good, wholesome people who simply lacked greater opportunity and went to Job Corps seeking for it.

Looking back, I long for the peace, fellowship, and simplicity that existed there. I was not prepared for that environment, and I admit I felt a little out of place. But I still felt a great urgency in my life. This urgency manifested itself as a spiritual impatience whose needs, I felt, could not be met in the middle of the forest.

As Christmas approached, I began to make plans to return to the coast to visit my father. I was able to spend the holiday with my dad and his wife. During my visit, I was able to visit with a few friends in my hometown.

Back with friends, we quickly began to make plans. I shared some of my thoughts and feelings and found a some comfort in getting "out of my head."

Within a short time, I found a job working as a maintenance man at a nursing home in Bellingham. With the purchase of a 1970's vintage 500cc Kawasaki motorcycle, I was set to re-establish myself. With a couple friends, I found a manufactured home for rent in northwestern

Washington, just south of the Canadian border. This home was nestled in a quiet secluded location, several miles west of the highway and just east of the coast.

However, my mind continued to be troubled. I sought for that truth I had known existed since my youth. How could the complexities of life be distilled into a single truth? Yet I believed it.

I found inspiration in music, poetry, and philosophical writings. As I tried to approach that great secret, I could feel the truth welling inside of me, looking for a voice. Guided by a feeling, a presence within that seemed to speak in riddles, I wrote poetry and prose, continually returning to my writings to riddle out the meaning.

I found myself sharing some of my thoughts, writings, and discoveries at a local coffee shop during their open mic night. My performances were received well, which gave me additional courage to continue in my pursuit.

While searching the writings of Plato, I discovered a passage from his *Symposium* that excited an aggressive thought process. This is a different translation, though will suffice for the illustration.

> Suddenly he will behold a beauty marvelous in its nature, that very Beauty, Socrates, for the sake of which all earlier hardships had been bourne: in the first place, everlasting, and never being born nor perishing, neither increasing nor diminishing; secondly, not beautiful here and ugly there, not beautiful now and ugly then, not beautiful in one direction and ugly in another direction, not beautiful in one place and ugly in another place....
>
> For let me tell you, the right way to approach the things of love, or to be led there by another, is this: beginning from these beautiful things, to mount for that beauty's sake ever upwards, as by a flight of steps, from one to two, and from two to all beautiful bodies, and from all beautiful bodies to beautiful pursuits and practices, and from practices to beautiful learnings,

so that from learnings he may come at last to that perfect learning which is the learning solely of that beauty itself, and may know at last that which is the perfection of beauty. There in life and there alone, my dear Socrates, said the inspired woman, is life worth living for a man, while he contemplates Beauty itself. (Plato's *Symposium*, Signet Classics, W. H. D. Rouse translation)

This passage, in conjunction with other thoughts and writings, had a profound effect on me. It helped me see the progression of what we term as love, which in fact is a pale imitation designed to teach us how to become our destined being.

I had finally approached that great secret, the knowing of which would connect all of the pieces. I was missing something but it would creep in, masking its entrance, like the dawn amidst the morning light.

Understanding the past,
explains the present,
hence dropping a bridge through war.
The true potential
of the future—
why didn't I see it before?

Years of turmoil,
trapped in a worldly strife.

To determine my peace,
I must submit to the weak,
and find my power in life.

But the power is His,
He has taken it away,
turning my peace to cease.

I will hold fast,
steady,
true,
He is my only release.

Amazing Grace

The urgency and foreboding continued until it reached what felt like a climax. My spirit was depressed, and work life was becoming increasingly strained.

Thoughts on beauty, love, and life swirled around in my mind. I was attempting to make the connection between eternal truth and the daily actions of mankind.

Agency, interpretation, and perception created a storm of options and possibilities. Why is the word love so widely used and abused? What gives it power? What takes its power away? I began to approach a thought, in degrees, starting at a trivial sentiment of appreciation, to a consumptive appetite, mounting ever higher to an appreciation of beauty beyond choice or desire.

When the power of Love
consumes multiple roots,
through the pursuit of Beauty
and each feels the power of the Source,
through the other,

a compelling urge to unite
inspires each interpretation of Beauty
to be an eternal intoxication.

Hence the desire for an everlasting communion.

At this time of great revelatory experience, in the early months of 1999, the Lord explicitly intervened on my behalf. Years of rebellion and confining pride were rooted from my breast and paraded before me in agonizing spiritual detail.

For three nights I was grappled by a spiritual aggression that left me writhing on the floor. It wasn't necessarily the pains of a damned soul so much as an exfoliation, removing the decay and selfish excess that had been hoarded over the years.

In hindsight, I believe it was a process of making the unknown known and bringing that which dwelt in darkness into the light. These evenings left me exposed in a manner that ultimately allowed me to assess myself and begin my recovery.

I was convicted by God and brought to acknowledge my destructive behavior. The chaotic, seemingly unstoppable, force that was my life came in contact with an immoveable object—truth.

I needed to get right with God and His law. My tendencies and temptations began to fade as I consciously chose to step away from my chains and placed them at the feet of Jesus. I started on my path to becoming my best self as I chose to accept the Grace of Jesus Christ in helping me overcome my temptations and weaknesses.

Unfortunately, in my spiritual immaturity, I was incapable of seeing, desiring, or addressing the full scope of my requisite growth and repentance. In time, the Lord would teach me my need and responsibility.

I began to see others in a different light. They were no longer objects to interact with or to extort. They were independent beings, children of an eternal God. I started to understand that I would be held accountable before God for my treatment of them.

My violent tendencies were tempered. I had gained a greater respect for the possessions of others, which respect only continued to grow. Lascivious pursuits and passions began to wane, though it took longer than I would have liked. Pornography and its ease to acquire made it extremely difficult. My addictions proved to be even harder to kick.

Alone, these obstacles would have seemed insurmountable. With Christ, and through His Grace, it was only a matter of time, dedication, and faith.

***

I was ashamed and I withdrew.

My motorcycle, job, and home were all broken or forsaken within a few days, and I was reduced to what I could carry on my back. The weight of my thoughts and experiences where too much for me to consume. I didn't have anyone whom I felt I could lean on to help me riddle out my experiences. I needed to decipher what I had learned, internally, in my mind and in my heart, therefore external needs were sacrificed. I felt an urgency that was difficult to shake.

At the age of 20, I found myself homeless. Hope was of the greatest worth to me. Not hope for my next meal or for a place to stay or any other creature comfort imaginable. The hope I sought was to have purpose, to belong, and to be valued.

When someone has nothing quantifiable (you be the judge of what that means), they might be led to wonder "what is the purpose of existing?" Sadly, I believe many individuals, trapped in despair, are saved only by their fear of death.

I had let go of or lost almost every possession I owned. But those are not the chains that held me bound, they only tightened the grip. Honest self-reflection, combined with a faith in Christ, proved to be the perspective that would carry me through.

The clarity of thought that accompanied those moments when I saw the world as it was, as if I didn't even belong to it, was truly liberating.

The time has come,
all roots to one,
and the heavens hold their stare.
United by Love, we battle the Beast,
dismantle the ugly chair.
Life is a book with only one rule,
Love is a skill to be learned.
A second chance, with no money to steal,
and only a bridge to be burned.

Freedom is—
a consciousness
that eludes us, so we cry.
Trapped by ourselves, in constant pursuit
of the Great American Lie.
The truth has been told: the Beauty we seek
dwells in the hearts of man.
So let go your restraints, plant your seed,
live God's beautiful plan.

Parting the sorrows
opens a door.
The great gates of Heaven;
He speaks, you hide.
He offers you purpose in life,
an escape from all the noise.
Let go of the earth,
open your soul,
live euphoric joy.

Arrogant Humility

In my searching, I sometimes found it difficult to discern between truth and error. I had for so long forgotten the voice of the Lord and become accustomed to indulgence that it was difficult to make the transition.

God had not left me, and He was ever ready to give me experience listening to the still, small whispering voice of His spirit. These opportunities came in both the form of guidance and the absence of guidance. In His silence, I could eventually learn to recognize my own influence and differentiate it from His voice.

My pride and the weight of my experiences left me with a feeling of obligation. Having separated myself from civility and responsibility, I found it difficult to identify my place in society. Even in the baseness of my circumstances, I felt an arrogant sense of purpose.

Having consulted the Lord in the matter, I felt impressed that my thoughts and experiences should be shared, though I believe I assigned a greater timing and magnitude than what the Lord had intended. I was not prepared, in any regard, to provide guidance for myself, let alone anyone else.

These feelings of obligation and purpose, as misguided as they may have been, put me on course for correction and progress. They provided the necessary catalyst to seek the Lord's will and instruction in my life. While the source of my intentions was flawed, the Lord turned the experience for my good.

I looked for Him. I diligently sought Him in my life. Even amongst my impious pursuits, the Lord walked with me, guiding me back to Him. Trajectory mattered most.

***

My efforts found many ventures. I determined to walk across the United States in a bid for attention. This thought was quickly rejected by the Lord, though not without significant effort on my part.

To establish this adventure, I asked a good friend to drop me off, high up a logging road in the western Cascade Mountains. From there I was intent on communing with the Lord before embarking on my grand mission.

I pled with the Lord atop the mountain, seeking His guidance and approval. I was met with anxiety, darkness, and rejection. As if that was not sufficient, ominous weather began to move in and I felt a certain uneasiness about my position.

Ultimately, I made the decision to abandon this pursuit, deeming my adventure unsanctioned and therefore unwise. I began the long descent down the mountain road. The weather's advance shadowed my retreat. The switchbacks in the road hindered the rate of my descent. I decided to abandon the road and find a more direct route off the mountain.

The thick tree cover made it impossible to adequately determine an ideal location for my detour. I calculated as best I could and made my turn. I began descending a steep slope, moving from tree trunk to tree trunk to provide sufficient opportunity for deceleration and redirection.

I descended along the side of a ravine carved out by a thin but established alpine stream. As I progressed in my course, the walls of the ravine continued to steepen. My footing became increasingly questionable so I moved closer and closer to the stream. My intent was to shorten the distance in the event that my footing gave way and I fell. This was rapidly becoming an inevitability.

Before long, I found myself mid-thigh in the cold mountain stream. I could no longer navigate the walls of the ravine and, by necessity, joined my path with the water. I was fortunate enough to be married to a stream that fell from the mountain by terrace. I preferred this over a high gradient continuous descent, a pool and precipice topography. It seems the roots, trees, and deadfall created a tortuous path that hindered the stream's progress but aided me in the management of mine.

Time, effort, and a lot of prayer brought me safely off the mountain. Drenched as I was, I secured a ride back to civilization through the kindness of a passing stranger.

***

Still caught up in my necessity, I looked for my voice. Hearing a song on the radio, I was impressed by the feelings it invoked. I had a love for music and its ability to stimulate the senses, to elevate the mind, and to enliven the soul. I felt this voice was worth investigating.

This particular voice, while not an avenue for expression, became an anchoring voice that continually persuaded me toward the light. Words of comfort and support helped to keep me going and fed my soul with hope.

With this hope came a hope for a better self. I was convicted and yet encouraged as I came to better understand myself. I continued to walk the path of introspection and correction as faith and repentance became my companion.

Slowly, an understanding formed. I believed that love and courage, and pride and fear, were the polar opposites influencing every decision I'd ever made. That great secret was contained within the power play between love and fear, as pride is only a bastardized imitation of love, and courage is an act of love under the influence of, and in spite of, fear.

***

Sleep became an ever-annoying event. Whether the fight was for location, acceptance, comfort, or safety, I was continually harassed by this dilemma. Often, I was blessed with the opportunity to find respite at a friend's house, in their car, or at my dad's studio apartment, which he used during the week for work. Other times I found myself in more creative situations.

Sleeping outdoors, begging the sun to rise as the morning mist chilled me to the bone, gave me a new sense of humility. The cold humid air of western Washington penetrated my clothing and caused great discomfort, encouraging despair. Fully aware of my pitiful plight, I felt terribly alone.

Approaching Desperate

In early July I was able to secure a ticket to a concert at the Gorge Amphitheater at George, Washington. I took a bus to George, though I did not have a way of getting to the amphitheater. I figured I'd just hitchhike like I had done many times before.

I arrived early in the day and was not able to find a ride down those country roads. It wasn't a loss though because the view was spectacular. I left the road for a short time and took some rest along the edge of the gorge, the large deep valley carved out by the Columbia River.

I ate a snack and changed clothes above the gorge, under a scrubby little tree. There was a certain freedom I felt atop the cliff, in the midst of rocks and bushes, surrounded by nature, returning to nature in the breeze.

Eventually I made my way to the Gorge Amphitheater. The area was designed to allow for campers since it was far from civilization, out in the desert. I set up my tent in a grassy field outside of the compound.

The concert went into the night, and I found myself disrupted by the entertainment. I was hoping for more substance than frivolous pandering, as I saw it. I realize that I was projecting my own thoughts and selfish desires on the artists. I didn't accept that sometimes entertainers only come to entertain, which is probably what most of the audience was anticipating.

I'm not exactly sure what I was expecting. Was I looking to go to a revival? Was I hoping for a political rally? While the music was deep and engaging, it was still tasked to entertain, which it did.

Following the concert, I returned to my tent to enjoy a good night's rest, devoid of judgment. I was in a place that I was supposed to be. I was just like everyone else. It is likely that few in the camp guessed my transient lifestyle.

My shame was left in town.

***

Later that summer a few friends and I decided to hike a sandy cliff, about 150 feet above the beach. We started along a path that led from the top of the cliff down to the beach. About 40 feet down, I stepped on a portion of the path that shifted underneath my feet. In that moment, I froze. A couple friends were with me, but I knew they could do nothing for me.

I looked at them and calmly said, "It looks like I'm going."

"What?"

"See you at the bottom."

The section of the path beneath my feet gave way. After falling several feet, I contacted a steep slope and began to tumble backward. While watching the ocean fly past my view repeatedly, I was tossed and battered against the cliff. As if in slow motion, the majestic evening view of the western water mingled with a peaceful yet astonished fear, creating a contrast which would imprint on my soul.

After being tossed against the cliff, I was able to arrest my revolutions and maintained a rapid slide on my belly. I reached out for what I could but only gripped a thin thorny vine, which ran through my fingers mockingly, leaving its mark in my hands.

Shortly afterward I was left clinging to air. I fell from some unknown elevation, though it felt to be substantial.

Landing on the rocky beach, I was "fortunate" enough to impact a log. I knew I had landed on a log because my head bounced. My ribcage, compressing on the log, was completely devoid of air. I emerged from the impact as if from the depths of the ocean, completely out of breath.

I grasped for air but only found a chirp. Floundering in panic, I removed one arm of my jacket in a futile attempt to assist in providing more air. Within a few minutes I was able to breathe, though it was labored and mingled with significant pain. I was assisted to the car by my friends, who took me back to my dad's apartment to sleep.

Though I may have broken a rib or two, I was unable to seek medical attention. I eventually recovered, though I certainly had a rough go at it.

Within two years, I had been attacked with a sword, wrecked my motorcycle, rendered myself homeless, and now the cliff dive. I was rapidly approaching desperate.

***

This was the summer of my twenty-first birthday. The elusive day arrived. The one I was not sure I would ever see. In the previous two years, if the Lord wished to take me, He had plenty of chances. Perhaps He intended for me to stick around a bit longer.

WTO

In November of 1999, tensions were high in the world and uncertainty was certain. While crossing Puget Sound aboard a ferry, I reviewed the tourist literature. Walk-on passengers tend to have a longer, more leisurely ride because the ferry is a short yet scenic experience and they are not burdened by filing in and out of vehicles and waiting in long lines to embark or disembark the vessel.

Filed amongst the tourist pamphlets were some amateur yet informative packets about an event that would shortly occur in downtown Seattle. The World Trade Organization (WTO) was having a conference and it had a lot of people stirred up.

The packet gave some brief explanations of a few of the many grievances placed against the organization and a schedule of informative meetings to be held during the time of and in close proximity to the conference. I decided this was an education worth pursuing, at least in part.

Returning to town, I proceeded to consult with a friend who had also determined this was a worthy pursuit and well worth the effort. It was decided that we would depart Tuesday morning in order to travel to Seattle for the Wednesday meetings.

The time for departure came but my friend was unable to go. Undeterred, I collected my backpack and boarded a bus for the ferry, alone. The journey aboard the bus and across the sound on the ferry was largely uneventful. After reaching shore, I caught a bus supposedly headed downtown. The bus driver informed me that all buses had been removed from downtown and were forbidden to return. I asked him to drop me off as close to my destination as possible. He stopped a few miles from downtown to let me off.

It was an eerie experience, walking the streets of Seattle. The once lively, active environment had been reduced to little more than a ghost town. Vehicles were scarce and humans were all but missing. About halfway on my pedestrian journey, I was passed by a young couple covered in pins and carrying a sign. Other than that, I cannot remember passing another soul before reaching downtown.

Late in the afternoon, the skyscrapers drew near. Finally, on the edge of downtown, I turned onto a street and saw an alarming site. From its base clear up to the top, the hill was teeming will people. Groups of individuals lined the street. Walking down the middle of the street, I passed them all, slowly making my way to the top.

About halfway up the street, I saw a most alarming and disturbing site. A group of individuals, dressed in black, baring the anarchist's brand, with faces veiled, were burning an American flag. Feelings of curiosity and wonder were now sharpened into alarm.

At the top of the hill, in the middle of the street, stood a stage with a group of individuals chained to it. Just beyond sat rows of protestors, and immediately past them stood a row of riot police in full riot gear. Lining the entrance to an adjacent street, stood an equally ominous looking barricade of riot police.

Time was far spent and the light was failing. At approximately 4:45 p.m., a young man mounted the stage to make an announcement. He informed all those within the sound of his voice that the police department had given an ultimatum to vacate the area by 5 p.m. He gave some very brief yet specific directions for the group to maneuver the streets down to the park, where they would all disperse. They would reconvene the next morning to continue their protest.

A request was made for assistance in relocating the stage to the sidewalk. Determined to help, I positioned myself at one edge of the stage, when I heard a strange noise, akin to a rush of pressurized air.

Looking up into the darkening sky, I saw sparks. Immediately following, a loud explosive sound occurred to my side and I felt something hit me in the cheek. As I recoiled to the side, a canister flew overhead, spewing a trail of smoke. The entire area immediately erupted into a scene of chaos and confusion.

I felt herded down the street to the west. Remaining calm, I raised my shoulders and lowered my head, using my backpack to shield the back of my head from any other projectiles, as I continued down the unknown street.

It should be noted, unknown to me at the time, the city had been plagued earlier that day by riots and looting. Shops had been ransacked and property damaged. Additionally, the unexpected advance of the riot police was most likely due to calculated disturbances caused by the individuals in black.

About halfway down the block I saw a large bottle flying through the air. The bottle hit its mark atop an urban riot tank. My alarm had reached a new height as my senses seemed to hone in to an acute awareness of my surroundings. The air was saturated by what can only be assumed to be tear gas; the smell of rubbing alcohol poured over fresh burning asphalt.

"By 5:00, large squads in riot armor and gas masks, backed by armored vehicles, began sweeping through downtown using concussion grenades, rubber bullets, and tear gas to force remaining protestors and bystanders alike off the street." WTO Meeting and Protests in Seattle (1999) — Part 2 (www.historylink.org/File/9213)

Miraculously, I was able to maneuver my way out of danger onto calmer Seattle streets. At this point, my mind turned to shelter for the evening. I learned that a tent city had been established elsewhere in the city as a safe haven for the homeless during this turmoil. Unaware of how to find it, I employed the help of a gentleman willing to lead the way. He was a rather kind man, who provided simple conversation while guiding my path.

My traveling companion, however, seemed to be troubled by some form of sinus disorder. He was continually attempting to evict some unwelcome occupant from his nasal cavity, and quite violently at times. I later discovered that the unwelcome guest was in fact a small balloon containing heroine, which he had conveniently lodged there for safekeeping. He was more than willing to share in this bounty, should it become available.

Finding ourselves at a convenience store, in which my companion needed to enter, I took the opportunity to take leave of my traveling partner, thanking him for his assistance and striking out on my own.

I eventually reached the tent city. It was located in a quaint little church parking lot atop a hill in the city. Very kind and attentive people were there to assist those in need. I was able to erect my small tent in the parking lot and was even provided some food. Throughout the night I could hear a small TV conveying the news from downtown, where individuals continued to confront police forces with primitive means. Helicopters filled the night air.

Sand Point

Early the next morning, after a brief interview with some of the volunteers at the church, I secured approval to leave my tent and belongings where they were. With a notebook in hand, firmly intent on attending the informational meetings I had come to attend, I set off for downtown.

After about an hour or so, I made my way up the street to the church where the meeting was to be held. The street and sidewalks were bustling with people on their way to work, conduct business, or shop. At first glance, the area seemed all but undisturbed by the previous day's activities.

About 9 a.m., and about a block away from my final destination, I rounded my final corner and was confronted by a police officer. Taking one look at me, my hair and attire, he estimated that I was an "undesirable" and should not be permitted to proceed, all while we were passed by multiple others who "appeared" to belong.

He questioned me about my business and purpose being downtown that morning. I informed him of my intention of attending informative meetings, pointing in the direction of my first destination. He adamantly insisted that I vacate the premises and abandon my immediate pursuits.

Having a difficult time processing his right to restrict my passage and prevent me from attending an informative meeting held in a church, I continued the discussion, attempting to persuade him to let me pass. Unknown to me, our dialogue and my continued attempts at persuasion seemed to irritate his colleague, who took matters into his own hands, blindsiding me into a wall.

Within a matter of moments, I was placed in handcuffs and escorted to the back of a police car.

"The following day, December 1, saw the illegalization of gas masks for the protestors and the creation of a 50-block "no protest zone" in the central business district. At the mayor's request, the Seattle police were joined by members of the Washington National Guard and the U.S. military. More mass dissension and acts of civil disobedience, some vandalism, and curfew violations resulted in reprisals by the police forces and the eventual arrest of more than 500 people on December 1 alone." www.britannica.com "Seattle WTO protests of 1999"

We drove around a block or two and then behind a police barricade. Parking on an eerily empty Seattle street, I was transferred into a police prisoner transportation van. I was accompanied by a couple other participants, one of whom reeked of marijuana. He disclosed that he had to consume his entire stash immediately prior to his encounter with the police. Looking out the back window, I saw in a side street, between a building and the walled drop-off to the Interstate (I-5), a tracked and turreted tank.

Eventually, we were ferried to an old abandoned military base at Sand Point. This base served as a processing point for the hundreds of people arrested on December 1st ("The Seattle Police Department After Action Report: World Trade Organization Ministerial Conference Seattle, Washington November 29 – December 3, 1999," p. 66). While some report the conditions were safe and hygienic, my experience was quite different.

After arrival and initial processing at Sand Point, I was placed in a large holding cell with several others. The room was composed primarily of concrete, with a few large windows along one wall. On the back side of the room were a few bathrooms and a drinking fountain, none of which were operational.

There were about 10 to 20 people in the room with me. Lacking anywhere else to sit, most or all sat on the floor. I remember several members of our group seated in a circle when a large man entered the room, flanked by others. He began to speak forcefully to us, demanding identifying information.

The group remained silent. Enraged by their continued protest, he grabbed the gentleman closest to the door by the collar at the back of his neck and drug him toward the door. The man remained in the seated position as his face changed several shades before finally being ejected from the room.

Eventually our cellmate was returned to us without any obvious significant harm.

Several hours following my initial detainment, I was placed on a prisoner transport bound for the King County Jail. This is where I was officially processed, with mugshot and fingerprints.

I was placed in another holding cell, much smaller than our last accommodations, though much cleaner. I was asked about my clothing and, after determining that I was wearing thermal underwear, was asked to relinquish my pants, to leave only one layer of clothing.

After noticing my lacking wardrobe, an officer called me over and provided me with the lower half of my prison uniform to conceal my shame. I was a bit self-conscious though, due to the fact that I found the lady officer quite attractive.

About this time (3:30 p.m.), I was finally able to secure a drink of water—my first drink since being detained earlier that morning. After I was fully processed, I was taken up several floors to my cell.

I was assigned a cell with a couple others caught up in the local festivities: a charming older gentleman from New England and a young long-haired gentleman with cosmetic bump implants in his forearms. These bumps were large at the elbow and progressively decreased in size toward his wrist.

Food was delivered about 5 p.m., and we spent the evening discussing the week's events and what had brought us to the neighborhood. That evening we heard of a large march in protest of the treatment of the hundreds of peaceful protestors arrested that day. Somehow, knowing of their efforts lightened and brightened my heart.

To my surprise, I learned that a friend of mine was detained in the adjoining cell. We briefly discussed our adventures through the food tray slots in our cell doors, before being shut down by an attending guard.

No Gas Mask

My quick and speedy arraignment was scheduled for early the next morning. I was placed in a holding cell outside the courtroom, with a handful of others awaiting our moment in front of the judge. I was soon taken into the courtroom and stood before the judge. Unknown to me, there was an adjoining room, behind glass, where members of the public could witness.

As the proceedings began, I was presented with a document and asked to sign it. I am still in possession of this document.

IN THE MUNICIPAL COURT OF THE CITY OF SEATTLE
KING COUNTY, WASHINGTON
City of Seattle, Plaintiff   Case No: 371975
vs   Incident No: 99-505131
John Mayhew, Defendant

On or about December 1, 1999, in the City of Seattle, King County, Washington, the above named defendant did commit the following offense(s):

Count 1
Commit the crime of failure to disperse by congregating with a group of four or more other persons and, there being acts of conduct within that group which created a substantial risk of causing injury to any person or substantial harm to property, refusing or intentionally failing to obey a public safety order to move, disperse or refrain from specific activities in the immediate vicinity.
Contrary to Seattle Municipal Code Section(s): 12A.12.020

Count 2

Commit the crime of pedestrian interference by intentionally obstructing pedestrian or vehicular traffic in a public place.
Contrary to Seattle Municipal Code Section(s): 12A.12.015(B)(1)

Count 3
Commit the crime of purchasing, selling, or possessing a gas mask in violation of Civil Emergency Order by knowingly failing or refusing to obey an order by the Mayor prohibiting the purchase, sale, conveyance, or transfer of any device commonly known as a gas mask after proclamation of a civil emergency or by knowingly failing or refusing to obey an order by the Mayor prohibiting the possession or carrying of any device commonly known as a gas mask in a public place after proclamation of a civil emergency.
Contrary to Seattle Municipal Code Section(s): 10.02.020(O) & 10.02.110
Dated: 12/2/1999

Assistant City Attorney
WSBA # 26016

Defendant Information:
JOSEPH HNERY PIECUCH - 372201
Address: TRANSIENT
Address: [ADDRESS LINE 2]
City/State/Zip code: [CITY_ST_ZIP]
Race: W   Sex: M   Birthdate: —/—/——
Height: 510"   Weight: 150   Eyes: Blue

Taking one look at the document and the gross inaccuracies within, I took a step backward, folded my arms, looked up, and refused to sign. Unknown to me, a photographer from the Seattle Post-Intelligencer snapped a photo of me, which would be printed in that Friday's newspaper.

I had been alone, did not obstruct vehicular or pedestrian traffic, and was not in possession of a gas mask at any time during the ordeal. They didn't even have the defendant information accurate at the end of the document.

At my protest, they removed me from the courtroom to discuss the situation in private. After deliberating for some time, I was asked to return to the courtroom. They had crossed out Count 1 and Count 3, and relabeled Count 2 to Count 1. They asked me, again, to sign the document. I refused again because the charge was completely false. After informing me that my signature was simply an acknowledgement that those were my charges, I conceded and signed their document.

I was returned to my cell to wait. Eventually, much later that evening and after dark, I was released on the condition that I would leave King County for a particular period of time and then return for a hearing later in December or January—when the charges were ultimately dropped.

I was in an unfamiliar part of town and had considerable distance to cover on foot before I had any hope of being reunited with my belongings, assuming they were still where I had left them after two days' absence.

Asking for directions and following the sub-gridded system of Seattle, I eventually found myself back in the church parking lot.

To my great surprise and relief, I found all of my possessions unmolested and cheerful faces welcoming me back. They expressed concern at my absence and interest in my adventures.

The next morning, in spite of my promise to leave immediately, I marched with thousands of others in a large protest against the World Trade Organization. I was still lacking the knowledge and information to sufficiently form an opinion for or against the WTO, though my participation in the march was more specifically a protest against the profiling and my subsequent treatment.

The march was filled with all aspects of society. It was a humbling melting pot of diversity collectively united in adversity. Protests ranged from imported steel to saving the whales and the turtles. Protestors' attire ranged from steel-toed boots to costumes and face paint.

During the march, I was approached by the photographer for the Seattle PI, telling me about the picture and soliciting my permission to publish. I was also approached by an affiliate of the ACLU who said she had witnessed my arrest and gave me her contact information in case I sought to pursue grievances. I lacked the energy, confidence, and desire to pursue the injustices, though I emerged from the ordeal with experience and greater perspective from all the interesting and amazing people I met and saw.

After the march, I was able to secure a ride to the ferry and return to my island. The lady who gave me a ride took me to Denny's for a meal. She told me of her desires for our nation's economic prosperity. She believed that the best political and financial scenario revolved around federal anarchy and a village/tribal social structure built from a barter system of trading goods and services.

I admit, this was a first for me. The lady was kind, articulate and seemed educated, yet she was expressing a concept that seemed so radical that it was hard for me to process. I have reflected on our discussion and I hope I can find understanding and humility as I accept that others may hold opinions that vastly differ from my own.

Busted

I was losing my safety nets. Friends were leaving or getting fed up. My dad had remarried and was giving up his studio apartment. At one point I was hanging out with a few acquaintances, drinking. It was getting late in the evening and I had nowhere I felt I could go.

With no other options, while sitting on the couch, I feigned sleep. In the midst of my pretended stupor, I overheard the discussion regarding how they could get rid of me. One of them would wake me, lead me out of the house, then, when in town, find a way to ditch me.

While this experience, in and of itself, was nothing special or unexpected, it showed me just how far I had fallen and how I measured up. I don't recall where I slept that night, if I slept at all.

***

Eventually, I got caught up again with drugs and their distribution. It seemed an easy way to obtain cash. As a distributor, I was suddenly interesting to other people. Those who wanted what I had to offer became my friends. I got lost in the situation and began to fall back into my previous deprivations and indulgences. Despair began to surface again and I lost all purpose and direction.

One evening while partying with friends, we got pulled over by the police. They found a glass pipe in my pocket, which led them to discover the marijuana on my person as well. As arrest seemed certain, upon finding the opportunity, I reached into my sock and retrieved my personal stash of acid (LSD). Applying it to my tongue, I guaranteed for myself an extremely stressful evening.

Tripping on acid while being booked and interrogated for drug charges (and trying desperately to not appear to be high), heightened my awareness and stress levels to near breaking points.

***

After being released, I took an offer to leave town and help tend a marijuana farm outside Eugene, Oregon. The grow location had not yet been established, so we loitered at the grower's apartment for a few days, while he prepared some starters.

Eventually, the grower drove me and another worker out to the forest so we could prepare the ground for the spring crop. He took us deep into the forest east of Eugene, up a hill from the road, just down from a major powerline thoroughfare. We set up camp engulfed in a thicket that masked us from view, both from the side and above.

My time in Eugene had given me an opportunity to reassess my situation. I had begun to contemplate life again, to use the quiet moments to reflect. I had wandered onto campus and conversed with a few Christian proselytes, which only increased my searching mind.

Away from all the noise, quiet in the forest, my mind and heart were heard again. Incessant and unrelenting, I was on edge and again burdened by urgency. So I left.

Jesus, Savior, Pilot Me

I packed up my things, hiked down the hill, and began to hitchhike east. I'm not sure where I ended up that first night. I remember finding a little rural town and taking refuge in a small public bathroom in a park. After locking the door from the inside, I attempted to sleep on the bathroom floor. Locking a public bathroom has a tendency to upset some people; one gentleman in particular was not impressed.

I was at the end of my rope and wanted to be secured behind a lock under my control.

The next morning, as I emerged and started my journey east, I was stopped by a police officer. Apparently, my warrant in Washington for skipping out on my court date hadn't registered in his system yet. He asked me where I was going, and I told him I was headed to Salt Lake City to look at the Mormon temple. He informed me that I needed some form of endorsement or certificate to go inside, but I didn't care.

He then offered me a ride to the east side of town. While this may seem like something out of a *Rocky* movie and that I was being oppressed, I didn't see it that way. I am unsure of the officer's intentions but, regardless, it is easier to get a long-distance ride from people leaving town than from those entering or traveling through town. So I took him up on his offer. I'm not sure exactly if I actually had a choice.

Somehow, I was able to secure passage to Ogden, just north of Salt Lake City. I slept under a bridge that night, high on a concrete shelf, far from lights and establishments. The only thing nearby was a KOA campground. Cold as it was in Utah in March, I slept peacefully.

The next morning, I hitchhiked further into town, though catching a ride becomes increasingly difficult in and around large cities. I found my way to a pawn shop where I tried to sell a compass drafting set, which I had taken from my dad. The owner wouldn't buy it from me, not trusting me of course. All I wanted was bus fare, so a young man there bought it off me for a few dollars, though the owner insisted we conduct the transaction outside.

After securing bus fare, I was able to catch a bus to downtown Salt Lake City. Loitering around the temple block, I observed the flowers and wandered around the grounds, just taking it in. I wasn't sure why I was there, though it felt right.

I entered a building where they were offering free viewings of a movie called *Testaments*. I went in and stood in line.

The building was ornate and immaculate. I was dirty, carrying a large backpack containing everything I owned. Others in line were laughing and conversing as if nothing was out of the ordinary, though I knew I was.

The movie was a powerful portrayal of Jesus Christ's visit to the Americas following His resurrection. I found it intriguing and moving. A particular scene struck me in which Christ healed the blindness of a man who had waited his entire life to see Him.

***

Following the movie, I attempted to secure a bed in the local homeless shelter, though I was turned away due to a lack of availability. I was saddened as I saw the pitiful condition of that part of town. The neighborhood appeared forsaken, akin to its residents. I believe I spent the night under the same bridge in Ogden.

***

After securing a Greyhound bus ticket from my dad, I ended up in a bus station in Boise, Idaho, looking for a ride back to the Pacific Northwest. It was late at night, and I was informed the station would be closed until morning. I stepped outside the door to a sound from across the street, "KILL THE HIPPIE." A group of skinheads took notice of me and thought I would be a great target for sport.

Upon re-entering the station, I asked an elderly couple for a few cents to help me obtain a locker for my backpack. They kindly agreed to my request, and I gratefully stashed my things and entered the cold night air to fend for myself.

The March night air was cold and uninviting. Setting out, I wandered, seeking security and warmth. As if by Providence from heaven, I found a knit pair of gloves, folded on itself, which lessened my discomfort and perhaps saved me from an unhealthy night on the streets.

Eventually, I curled up under a bush, void of any foliage, begging the sun to rise.

Arising from the cold hard ground, at the first indication of morning's light, I began to wander, hoping to encourage life to return to my extremities.

I encountered a couple more homeless individuals. Interesting characters—one of which seemed almost proud to be homeless and acutely aware of how to meet his needs.

They led me to a church where a free breakfast was being served. Delicious pancakes with the works.

I asked if I could help clean up but they declined my offer. I understood their desire to serve and provide means for those who have so little, though, in situations akin to mine, an opportunity to return an act of service, to give back, have purpose, to contribute, could have meant more to me than the meal. To be looked at as someone who had something to offer, to be valued for my contribution, could have been a powerful moment in my life. Either way, I appreciated their sacrifice and service and accepted it gratefully.

My guides then led me to a food line where I was able to secure bread, peanut butter, honey, and a pound cake. This food would serve me for the next few days and keep me until I got where I needed to go.

***

My departure from Boise occurred later that day, and I rode all the way to Portland, Oregon, where I met up with a friend of mine in Gresham.

Hitting a wall, I broke down and called my mom. We had not spoken for a couple of years. She was living in western Colorado at the time and said that I could come live with her for a while. Shortly afterward, I began a long hitchhike, eastward again.

East to Colorado

After fashioning a sign out of cardboard, I posted up in front of a gas station in Gresham, Oregon, looking for a ride.

While I waited, I began to read a bit in the scriptures. Fortunately, this attracted a couple long-haul truck drivers, who gave me a lift. They later remarked that when they saw me reading the scriptures they thought I couldn't be all bad.

We traveled for a while through the Columbia River Gorge. About dinner time, we stopped at a diner. They offered to buy me dinner, but I told them, in my ignorance, that I was fasting on bread. I think I just wanted time to sit and think on my own. I hiked up a hill next to the diner, sat down, and enjoyed the solitude.

We ended up at a truck stop in Idaho at the end of the day. They let me out of the truck and told me that if I was still there in the morning, they would continue to give me a ride toward Grand Junction, on the western border of Colorado.

That evening I was unsuccessful securing a ride, so I slept on the grassy slope of the on-ramp, waiting for the sun to rise.

Sometime between first light and sunrise, I awoke and resumed my position at the on-ramp of the interstate. Within a short time, I was picked up by a large man in a semi-truck.

This man was interesting and intimidating at the same time. He seemed kind and engaging. He was headed out to the east coast, down

Interstate 80, and was going to drop me in northern Utah to finish my journey.

By the time we reached the turn-off, he had offered me work. I was going to head out east with him, where I would help him with his deliveries. He promised to drop me off on the return trip.

He told me about his service in the Vietnam War and his time spent in a POW camp. His hardships and those of his fellow prisoners were greatly compounded by an informant among his companions.

He showed me a large scar on the side of his face, which he attributed to a rod being thrust through his head while in the camp. He also confessed to me that he had participated in the execution of the informant, once he was discovered.

About this time, I started to become uneasy with my situation and commitment. Eventually, I convinced him that I would not be joining him and would prefer to head back to Colorado.

He dropped me off in Cheyenne, Wyoming, and helped me secure a ride to Denver with another trucker. Late that night, I was eventually dropped off in Denver. About two miles east of the I-25 / I-70 interchange, I found myself looking for another ride, just outside a Pilot truck stop.

Because I was unsuccessful obtaining transportation during the night and morning, I moved out to the road from which I saw most of the trucks leaving. Sometime around noon, a trucker on his way in told me he would give me a ride if I was still there when he came back out in a couple of hours.

Sometime following this, I was offered a ride by a European gentleman and his daughter. They were only going as far as Golden, which wasn't far, but it got me out of downtown and on the west side of Denver. I took the ride without hesitation.

It was a short but pleasant ride. My hope was renewed as I got further out of town. The further from downtown I was, the easier it was to get a ride.

Shortly after they dropped me off, I secured a ride up the east slope of the Rocky Mountains to Vail. My host was a younger man with a 4-Runner-type vehicle, who obviously enjoyed the outdoors. We had a good refreshing discussion for an hour or so, until I was dropped off at a little grassy turn-around in Vail. In the middle of the grassy area, was an enclosed "Superman style" phone booth and several large rocks.

At this point I was so exhausted that I called my mom and asked her to come get me. Little did I know, she was still about three to three and a half hours away, and she had to wait until she got off work. Comfortable in my surroundings, I sat and nodded in and out of consciousness as I watched the snow crawlers move across the slopes above, seemingly adjusting the snow pack to avoid uncontrolled avalanches.

Some hours later, I was reunited with my mother in the cold dark evening of Vail in March. It was Good Friday, 2000.

Prodigal Son

After about a year of being homeless, I found safety in my mother's home, friendship with a young family, and spiritual leadership in my local church.

Friends who were honest yet reserved judgment have been indispensable to my continued growth. Never underestimate your ability to do good or to affect positive change in the lives of others.

Loneliness manifests itself in more than just those without social companionship.

The damage caused by my years of indulgence and rebellion was not easily overcome. I was ignorant of many things that seemed to come naturally to most people. My progress was not always progress. I hoped to appear well-adjusted, but at times I was, at best, socially awkward (though often ignorant of my behavior or how it was perceived).

At other times, I would struggle with a lack of vision and deep seeded self-worth insecurities. These struggles could reproduce loneliness and despair, with its destructive yet comfortable familiarity.

I soon found work on a dude ranch on the edge of the Blue Mesa Reservoir. I helped take care of the horses, lead trail rides, and slept in a bunkhouse. I tried to find my responsibility to myself and to God. It was difficult to navigate my needed growth, though the seclusion in nature certainly helped.

The family who hired me, though unaware of my circumstances, was very kind and helpful. I wasn't sure what I wanted or how I was going to accomplish it if I ever figured it out. I was living day-by-day and, at that time, it was good enough.

Drug abuse, combined with a lack of appropriate healthcare and hygiene, was extremely destructive to my teeth.

My wisdom teeth had started to come in several years prior. At least one on the top was impacted below the gum line and was rubbing against my back molar. The two lower wisdom teeth compressed between my back molars and my jaw bone, crushing my lower teeth together. Cavities formed on two of my premolars. As my wisdom teeth came in, they pushed the adjacent teeth into the cavities, continually aggravating the wounds.

One evening at the ranch, one of my damaged premolars broke in half. I spent the night sitting atop the hill outside the bunkhouse, staring at the mares, again, waiting for the sun to rise. Excruciating pain robbed me of sleep and all I could do was wait.

The next morning, I called my mom and secured a ride home for that evening. Unable to focus, I was next to useless the entire day. Once my mom arrived, I sat in the back of the truck with my mouth open because the cool night air was the only thing that seemed to help.

Over-the-counter medication had no effect, so I spent that evening waiting for tomorrow. The next day while at a neighbor's house, I was offered some leftover prescription medication. I gratefully accepted and within minutes fell asleep in the lawn chair in the front yard.

A member of our local church was a dentist. He offered to perform the extractions and only charge me for the anesthetic and maybe the x-rays.

Soon, I was taken in for surgery and placed under general anesthetic. All I remember is the nurse telling me a joke as she stuck me with a needle. I passed out while laughing.

They removed all four wisdom teeth, two premolars, a molar from above that had formed a serious cavity against a wisdom tooth, and an adjacent molar that had dropped its filling and cracked in half due to the compression. I discovered that they broke them to get them out, as I found a large sliver of tooth in my gums a few days following the surgery.

I ended up leaving my first ranch job and took another that was located east of Meeker. We had to drive several miles down a dirt road, then pack a couple miles up a trail with horses and mules to reach the lodge. It was a small hunting cabin that we were preparing for the upcoming season.

The cabin had several bunks, an outhouse, and a stove. The shower was located in a small log hut that was comprised of a hard floor and a wood stove. We heated up water on the stove in a bucket with a shower head attached to it. We would then hang it from a hook and turn it on intermittently so we could stay damp and to remove the soap after washing.

The other ranch hand was an older, weathered fellow. He was difficult to please.

While in the mountains, I took the opportunity to commune with God. One night, during a storm, I pled with God to direct me. I have often felt closer to God during storms.

The following day, I was thrown from a large Percheron mare. She spooked, then just as I was recovering my balance, she stopped, sending me flying over the horn. I landed with the middle of my back on a rock that was protruding out of the ground.

My time in those woods was brief. I gave up on my grumpy companion and returned to Grand Junction, where I got a graveyard shift stocking pallets at Sam's Club. The night team was a great crew and we had a good supervisor.

Early in August, I took a Greyhound bus to southern California to see another concert. It was in an attractive little park in San Juan Capistrano, and was preceded that morning by a horse show. The area was beautiful and clean.

After the concert, undeterred, I slept under a thinning bush near the area where I was going to be picked up the following day. The street lights were an annoyance, though the worst part was the sprinklers that woke me up in the darkened hours of the morning.

The Clouds of Night's Darkness Are Fleeing Away

I was experiencing growth in all facets of my life. Spiritual leadership from my local congregation helped me on my path of repentance. I was not fully aware what that meant or what was required. It was an extremely difficult process.

Lasciviousness, abuse, and criminal behavior had filled much of my teen years. Convicted in my heart, I sought to repent and correct my behavior as my conscience became sensitive through spiritual prompting.

Perfect love casts out all fear. Where fear and doubt are, love and faith are stifled.

The cleansing power of the atonement of Jesus Christ must be applied in humility and contrition to have maximum effect. Try as I might, my fear kept making it "about me."

During this process, though before the depth of my betrayal was fully apparent, my bishop asked me if I had considered serving as a missionary. This thought intrigued me and truly felt like the right thing to do, though the path to becoming that person seemed daunting. Diligently and lovingly, my bishop never wavered in his assistance. For this, I am eternally grateful.

I still struggled with marijuana, though, for some unknown reason, it didn't seem to register with me that it was illegal and needed to be abandoned. While having a conversation with someone a couple months later, he pointed this fact out explicitly, and I never touched the stuff again.

In hindsight, this is particularly odd to me as I still had a warrant for my marijuana charge in Washington. I realize that choice is a particular player in this and helps me to understand why we cannot be saved in ignorance. I needed to acknowledge the full weight and consequences of my actions and then decide. I truly wanted to be a good person, to obey God's law and the laws of man. Caught in my addiction and my need, I failed to see drugs for what they were.

***

The next obvious step in my growth and progress involved clearing up my warrant in Washington. Getting right with God and His law requires, of necessity, that I get right with the laws of man.

Sometime in early December, I quit my job at Sam's Club, determined to turn myself in. My mom drove me about an hour west to get outside of town. It was snowing very hard that day and was near whiteout conditions, though the wind was not blowing very hard.

She dropped me off at the on-ramp at Crescent Junction, Utah. She stopped for gas and I had a ride before she returned to the highway. That night, I was able to take refuge under my favorite bridge in Ogden, Utah, right down the road from the KOA campground. With the snow piling up around me, I was comfortable in a new sleeping bag and the warmth in my heart from knowing I was on the path of repentance.

The next day I was able to get to Baker City, Oregon, where I secured a seat on a Greyhound bus bound for Seattle. I ultimately arrived in my hometown, where I submitted myself to the law. I found myself in front of a judge who gave me a little time in jail, a fine, and about six months' probation.

On this trip, I was able to spend some time with my aunt, uncle, and cousins in Bellevue, and a friend in the Portland area. In Portland, I followed my friend into establishments where the spirit was not likely to follow, though I did so thinking I was strong enough to withstand those temptations. Those memories are still with me, and I wish I had not gone.

Shortly after returning home, around New Year's Day, I received a phone call from my bishop asking me if I was afraid of electricity. Unknown to me, he owned an electrical business. He offered me a job as an electrician's apprentice, which I gladly accepted.

My experience as an apprentice has given me many memories and lessons that have followed me throughout my life. This also gave me the opportunity to quickly pay off my fines and prepare to serve a mission.

Finally, the day came when I could submit my application to serve as a missionary for my church. It felt good to be at a point where I could comfortably put my name out there in such a capacity.

I was moving myself and my self-image away from my past. Shame and guilt encouraged a facade that avoided giving away any clues about my earlier years. I also considered this typical and desirable for someone who had forsaken their sins.

In some ways it only masked the damage. In other ways it masked my identity.

No amount of shame or displeasure can separate me from my choices and experiences. If I wanted to distance myself from the person I once was, I needed to embrace my experiences and learn all I could to become better, stronger, and wiser; confess them and forsake them.

This lesson does not come easily.

I was called to serve in a Las Vegas mission. I spent most of my time up north in Reno, Sparks, and Carson City, though I did spend several months in Summerlin, on the west side of Vegas.

What an amazing experience. I had the great honor and privilege to represent the Savior of mankind and teach His truths and redemption to His children. I was blessed in my position to serve on His behalf.

My mission was not without its struggles. I made many mistakes and fell into various temptations from time to time. Nothing serious, as I truly wanted to serve honorably, but I had moments of weakness when I wasn't as valiant as I ought to have been. Again, another lesson I continue to learn.

As much as I wanted to escape my past, some things couldn't be avoided. I didn't have a driver's license and couldn't get another one without special, expensive insurance. With the help of mission leadership, I was able to get my driver's license while in Las Vegas.

I had never graduated from high school, though I had earned a GED previously. While in Las Vegas I started to pursue the crazy idea that I might be able to attend college. I made plans to take the ACT (college entrance exam) so I could apply. It had been several years since I had attended school and, even when I was there, I hadn't paid much attention. I wasn't sure what the ACT was going to ask. I was woefully unprepared, though I felt somewhat optimistic.

So one morning I went to a local high school, dressed in my missionary suit, and took the ACT with a bunch of high school juniors and seniors, while my companion locked himself in the car. With a decent ACT score and recommendations from my mission leadership, I was able to secure a spot in college.

After completing a two-year mission, I returned to Colorado, spent a couple months working, got a car and drove to school in Idaho. I was attending a church school with high standards for dress, grooming, and morality. I felt additional pressure to move further and further away from my "former" life.

I was compelled to cover my tattoos if I wanted to wear a short-sleeved shirt. I used a thick sweatband to hide the tattoos on my forearm. I thought it looked okay, but others thought I was trying to make a fashion statement.

I entered college completely unaware of my potential. When I declared my major, I chose photography because it interested me and I felt I didn't need a lot of educational background to compete. My first math class was about the simplest class I could find, 100B. Lucky for me, I ended up being pretty good in math, so I minored in it and went on to graduate school to study geophysics.

After my mission, I started to think about dating again. I met many beautiful, amazing women, some of whom seemed to take an interest in me. Our relationship would progress while we talked about the now and the future, though as thoughts and discussions ventured toward my past, I became nervous and distant. I did not feel comfortable sharing that aspect of my life with anyone, let alone someone who had an emotional gateway to me.

Toward the end of my second semester, I met a beautiful young lady. We talked often and began to date just before the break. We remained in communication almost daily while apart. This long-distance relationship may have given me the courage to open up to her. She reserved judgment and accepted me for who I was. We were married about four months later.

After exploring several different majors, I settled on geology. The professors, staff, and students were fantastic. Their kindness, assistance, and encouragement helped me through.

***

Between my junior and senior years of college, I participated in a research internship funded by the National Science Foundation (NSF). This was a rewarding and extremely challenging experience. We were researching the tectonic strain experienced along the Norumbega Fault on the east coast of Maine.

We kayaked between islands, camping on the islands during the week and returning to the University of Southern Maine (USM) campus on weekends to do laundry and resupply. While on the islands, we mapped the area using total stations and real-time kinetic (RTK) GPS units.

We were particularly interested in the deformed granite intrusions. We used the deformation patterns to back calculate the strain along the fault since the intrusion occurred.

Following the field study, we returned to the USM campus to evaluate our observations and prepare posters to present at a conference later that fall in New Hampshire.

Academically, this was an experience of a lifetime. Emotionally and spiritually, it was a tumultuous roller coaster. This was the first time I had been away from my wife for an extended period since our marriage. It was also the first time in several years I had been exposed to such a level of temptation.

I found myself becoming guarded and angry. Several of my colleagues were prolific drinkers, and some were vulgar and uncouth. I had had a tendency to behave in a similar fashion, only worse, and I became rather judgmental against their behavior, thinking myself better and beyond such behavior. I was not prepared or confident enough to let them be as they were.

I was exposed to my weaknesses on several fronts, and I found the revelation to be extremely depressing. My research companions and professors were kind and accommodating. They were unaware of my inner turmoil and put up with my difficult behavior better than would be expected.

***

Throughout my time as a geology student, I took up rock and mineral collection. I was fascinated by the knowledge I was gaining and wanted to have a collection of my own. I also had hopes of teaching some day in the future and thought a diverse rock collection would help me in that endeavor.

In my search for more rocks, I had little respect for where I was while collecting. I collected rocks from the roadside, in the mountains, along public lands and parks, and even on the islands of my internship. At the time, I didn't give much thought to the ownership of small rocks, though this disregard for the property of others or the inappropriateness of the location brought me great shame later. I was ashamed that I could be so weak and selfish after all that the Lord had taught me and the great blessings of His mercy.

This revelation caused me to be even more guarded about my behavior and what I deemed to be acceptable.

***

Just prior to graduation and moving on to graduate school in San Diego, my wife became pregnant with our first child. When we arrived in San Diego, my wife had to obtain California state healthcare because my school coverage had not yet kicked in. She had a pre-existing condition, pregnancy. Even though we had healthcare in Idaho, it didn't count.

She found a doctor she liked, and when the school healthcare took over, we thought it would transfer. A couple of days prior to delivery, we learned the insurance wouldn't cover the doctor visits. Her doctor was amazing and generously lowered her fees as far as she could, but it was still a sizable amount.

So within a matter of days, my wife went to a new hospital, met a new doctor, and had a Cesarean birth. Our daughter was born halfway through my first year of graduate school.

Think of Me Thou Ransomed One

I'd been checking the boxes of progress and commendable life living. College, marriage, child... now what?

I missed the mark. In hoping for and actively pursuing these worthy goals, I assumed my becoming would occur naturally. I associated my character and self-worth with these accomplishments and missed the deeper meaning in my pursuits.

I began to suffer bouts of anxiety. With the economic crash in 2008, neck-deep in my thesis, and a new baby in our family, it was easy to feel overwhelmed. I was having a hard time understanding what I needed to do to complete my thesis, and I just wanted it to be done with. I found myself trying to do the minimum and convince myself and my advisor that I had gained sufficient knowledge, at least to a passing level, though I hadn't gained the depth I probably should have in all areas.

I found seclusion and escape in an online video game. It was easy to hide from life and responsibilities when I got caught up in fantasy. My life suffered as a result. My wife suffered, my schooling suffered, and my children suffered. I stopped believing that my life had meaning and purpose. I was sad and complacent.

In spite of this, I was fortunate enough to receive a very good job offer from an oil and gas company in Houston, Texas. It was not the field I was hoping to pursue, but with the economic crash and significant student debt, for myself and my wife, I couldn't refuse it.

In July, after some additional work following my defense, my advisor allowed me to graduate. This required a few revisions to my thesis and then submitting it to a journal for review.

I told my advisor that I would help with the edits once they returned from the reviewers. I assisted for a while but ended up handing it back to him, taking a backseat to the published credentials.

Shortly after our move to Houston, my wife became pregnant again, with our first son. This pregnancy was a much different experience as we had resources and insurance to ensure optimal healthcare for mother and child.

My new job sent me all over the world. Within the first few years, I spent significant time in Europe and Canada and even ventured to other places such as Ghana, Australia, Singapore, Vietnam, and Brunei.

It was difficult to adjust to corporate life. Many of my thoughts and ideas belonged to someone else. I continued to struggle with authority and the idea that my technical work and discoveries only carried the value that was assigned to them. I had to learn to let go and understand that the thoughts that were of greatest value to me could not be owned by another.

One of my greatest struggles and weaknesses has been my defense and coping mechanism for dealing with spiritual or intellectual conflict. I have often been ridged in my application of perceived truth and understanding. Certain that my inflexibility is perceived as self-righteousness, I believe I have offered offense and turned some people away.

It may not be apparent to others, and even myself at times, that this rigidity was a defense mechanism and sometimes a cover to mask insecurity and shame, and also a guard against further deception or temptation.

At times my behavior was self-righteous, though this too was a defense and did not stem from a solid footing upon moral high ground.

***

Throughout my travels and time in Houston, I was continually embroiled in a battle between arrogance and despair, and this fight often manifested itself in the form of depression, guilt, and self-loathing. I continued to retreat and step away from God. I stopped caring and thinking I mattered in this world, ignorantly telling myself that this was an appropriate way to address my arrogance.

One night, on a flight to Singapore, the adversary took my proclivity for guilt and self-loathing and buried me, again, in despair. I felt the weight of all my sin, temptations, and weaknesses return to me in full measure. This was unlike anything I had experienced previously. I was at my limit and I was alone, desperately and miserably forsaken.

Ignorant as I was, I focused on my faults, unable to give them to the Lord. I allowed my sins to take new holds upon me as I feared how others might respond to knowledge of my past.

My guilt and pain had little to do with what I did to myself. The drugs, and alcohol, while devastating in their effects, paled in comparison to my behavior toward others. My soul was especially assaulted because of my violence, selfishness, and the way I had treated God's daughters. I was powerless, ashamed, fearful, and self-despised.

God withdrew His spirit from me, though I implored for its return. I was depressed, lonely, and dejected. Church leaders could offer little help. I felt like my prayers were heard but ignored. My ignorance regarding the Lord's infinite and eternal sacrifice facilitated a depression and deprecation that hindered my ability to see my path to becoming. I did not have the faith necessary to find peace and confidently move toward a productive, contributing life.

My desires for all good things in life all but vanished. My hopes and dreams seemed to fade from view and I just wanted it to end. Thoughts of suicide were no comfort, for I knew my trial would only follow me and perhaps even seal itself to me in the act. I had to bear it patiently, or as patiently as I could.

***

Walking in
my pondered thoughts,
I stop to hear the rain.
Awakening my inner self,
I've found the prize to claim.

Revelation fed my soul;
I felt a beauty sweet.
I plucked the lion
of my heart,
and prayed myself complete.

A missing piece was later found
that led me to this place.
A fruit so strong
that fell with night
but was familiar to the taste.

Perspective, reason,
and a love
that I alone can't see,
communicate
your gentle faith
then you will complete me

Years before, I had sought for truth; unmasked, unapologetic truth. I believed that there was a single, simple truth that contained all truth, upon which all other truth was built. I had determined that this truth which contained all truth could be found in deciphering the elusive and often abused concept of love. A word with such depth and breadth that it spans from the basest superficiality to the greatest connection, for which we have no language to express.

I actually believed that I could discover this truth, though I had all but forgotten and given up on that sentiment.

Early in November 2011, in Bandar Seri Begawan (Darussalam: "abode of peace"), Brunei, in my pleading heart, the Lord showed me the meaning of love and that God is love, through the atonement of his Son, Jesus Christ.

While the initial effects of this experience were spiritual and significant, I did not fully understand the import of this revelation.

***

My healing continued to be hindered in its progress by my fear. I sought to control God's dealings with me and to set bounds on my repentance. Submission and acceptance of the Lord's Grace was my only path to release.

The pain and suffering originating from my actions also rippled through eternity, causing the Son of God excruciating pain. Only through the Savior could I hope to find peace. Jesus Christ is truly hope for the hopeless.

He is My Salvation From Sorrow and Sin

Those whom the Lord loves, He chastens. Is chastisement punishment? It is far more than that. Chastisement is intent on correction. The Lord loves me, so He wishes to correct my actions and put me on a course to eternal truth and, from there, on to live in His presence.

Why is chastisement required? To ensure I am sufficiently humble to receive the correction. Truth revealed often requires me to redefine what I thought to be true. That redefinition may even require a change in some aspect of my life that I considered to be character defining, a piece of myself that without which I would (in some way) become less than what I was before. That change hurts.

I must be humble. If I am not humble, I may (and in all likelihood will) reject the revealed truth and therefore find myself under condemnation, thus thwarting the Lord's plan and intention from the beginning.

He gave me "line upon line, precept upon precept, here a little and there a little," according to the heed and diligence that I showed to Him and His promptings. For with the chastisement the Lord prepared a way that I might be delivered in all things out of temptation.

***

I found some comfort in doing good, though I did not find a discernible measure of the Spirit there. In the depths of my despair and the loss of all my desires and earthly pursuits, I learned a few lessons. I was left with God's will for me, and I was taught what things in life truly matter to me. I needed to learn how to love and forgive myself.

Ultimately, I felt the need to sacrifice my will to God's will. In doing this, I found myself in a hole. I found it hard to ask God for things that I wanted, as I had all but lost hope in my ability to discern God's will for me, due to my arrogance and lack of understanding of His purposes for me.

Years later, I realized that instead of giving my will to God, I was, in part, blaming Him for my heartaches, struggles, and unmet expectations. I had called it "His will" instead of my will aligned with His. I began slowly, trying to embrace God's purpose for me and see His hand in my life as I owned my situations and circumstances, desirable or not.

***

I still remember the first time I was able to acknowledge the influence of the Spirit during this struggle. It was through a very simple act of a friend who said he saw goodness in me.

At that moment, the Spirit crashed upon my soul as the waves of the sea against the rocks upon the shore. I was overcome with a comforting peace that washed over me. I have grown since these experiences, though they have not completely left me. They serve as a reminder of my need to be humble, grateful, and forgiving.

***

If I could but separate my experiences from how I chose to respond to them, I could own my influence and others' influence on me. I could recognize how the adversary infiltrates my life, at the core, and combat it.

Everyone experiences significant negativity in their lives. Some of this negativity comes from external influences, some originates from within. Individually and collectively, we can see everyone as independent individuals consumed by their perception of reality.

I hope to use my influence to buoy up and to encourage decisive action and honest introspection, to separate our experiences, feelings, opportunities, and circumstances from how we chose to respond to them. To act, encourage action, and not be acted upon is true freedom. We have the power to choose.

I continue to fight against my natural self, to overcome my unhealthy desires and weaknesses, though I do not do it alone. I am yoked with Christ in carrying life's load. His mercy and Grace enable me in my righteous pursuits.

Friends and family continue to help along the way. Honesty about my struggles and shortcomings helps to foster trust and patience. I serve the Lord and His children where I can and how I can. I serve in my local church and my community.

Though my natural self continues to rebel, I move forward and act. As I have strength to proceed, I slowly step forward and command my natural self to step backwards. It is not always easy, and I do make several mistakes, though it is the trajectory that is the most important.

Jesus Christ suffered all, that I might be forgiven, if I would repent and come unto Him. In Him and through Him I can do all things which are according to His will. It is His will that I participate in the blessings of His atoning sacrifice.

Every life has purpose.

No one in this life is out of reach of God's mercy and love. It has always been so, and we can discover how that is possible.

Awaken hearts,
feed their souls,

Take the oath,
renew the old.

A tarnished past
hinders growth
if lies cover tears.

Faith in God
and Love for Christ,
can wipe away your fears.

Pride of heart
empowers the mind,
yet starves the living soul.

Open your heart,
give of yourself,
and make diamonds out of coal.

PART II – GRACE

Moral Agency

God wants me to be happy. I've learned that this happiness, a deep and abiding joy, must stem from within and be independent of all temporal things, else my happiness will be temporal too. And, with all temporal, earthy things, they are temporary.

To find true, independent, abiding happiness I must want it, seek it and own it. That ownership does not mean I can wrap it up, put it in my pocket, and call on it whenever I desire. It means that when I act, and claim my life, I will develop a character based on the dictates of my own conscience. My character will define my happiness.

We are all different. That is part of God's plan for us. An essential aspect of eternal happiness is independence. The Light of Christ is given to all born into this world so that we may know good and evil. Regardless, I have the opportunity to ignore that light and mold my perception of good based on my personal wants and desires.

I am an agent unto myself.

As an agent, I am given the opportunity to choose. To choose is to deliberately own, accept, receive, and sustain as an act of will with purpose, committed to action. Choices can be made from or in spite of external situations or stimuli, though, when made, they no longer depend upon those initial factors. They stand alone upon their own merits, else I am setting a priority, conducting an experiment, or responding circumstantially.

I can choose in a way that is empowering, and enlightening; the choices that are born from a marriage of my heart and my mind;

choices that stem from belief and give purpose in faith. My choices are a vehicle for defining who I become.

I must stand up and take control of my life, no longer allowing myself to be moved and swayed with every new thing that comes along or to commit my life to mediocrity. To spend my strength for that which does not satisfy. To give value to that of no worth.

***

I am a moral agent; I think and choose for myself. I have the power to become. My growth and becoming is governed by the truth I receive, honor, and own. Experience has taught me that every choice has consequences that ripple into the future.

Which future?

Eternity!

One of the founding principles in God's plan for my becoming is that I have the ability to act for myself, to triumph over my weaknesses or to succumb to them. I become as I own my choices and act according to the truth I have received.

Action is not always an observable act. Every choice I make is an act of becoming.

I am unable to predict, control, or alter aspects of this world that are consequential to my existence. However, I am empowered to choose how I respond. In choosing, I own the consequences as an opportunity to learn, choose again, and grow.

I am not a victim!

I am not an object to be acted upon!

I am a child of Almighty God.

I am an eternal being and life will continue beyond this veil of tears. Through the atonement of Jesus Christ, I will be resurrected, reunited with my body in an immortal state, never to be separated again.

What will that body be like?

That body will be a perfected, glorified version of the person I choose to become. This is accomplished through the resurrection of Jesus Christ and my use of the moral agency which the Lord has given, that I may be accountable for my own actions in the Day of Judgment.

My spirit and body are impacted by my choices. The glory I attain to in the eternities will be in the likeness of the person I chose to become, based on the heed and diligence I have given to eternal principles.

My choices beget more choices. Refusing to choose and allowing myself to be acted upon by my natural self or circumstance forfeits my innate ability to spiritually connect with the consequences. Being governed by my natural self limits my ability to make correct choices later, through desensitization, addiction, or physical, spiritual or emotional imbalance.

Avoiding choice also affects my fundamental ability to recognize and accept truth, or the Light of Christ. The more I turn away from or ignore truth, the faster that Light, or the acknowledgment of that truth, fades from me.

Correct choices made outside of my natural self, often in spite of my natural self, free me from my natural self.

When decisions and actions are forced upon me, regardless of their merits, I can easily become embittered by them. Then, even if the outcome of these forced decisions is good, or result in a good gift being given (service, kindness, etc.), I end up giving the gift grudgingly. I then forfeit the positive consequences of becoming from the act of giving because I do not internalize the benefits and merits of giving such a gift. Then when the opportunity arises for me to give willingly, I may be inclined to say, "I have already given, and it is enough." I therefore condemn myself the second time.

When conflict occurs (between choices), the fundamental belief system that governed those choices is challenged (belief, principles, doctrine). There arises a need to discover the root of the conflict and then resolve it. This has been one of the most uncomfortable yet rewarding aspects of my life.

Conversely, I have also been offended by these conflicts. For years I adopted the mentality of "I don't care." I felt that this perspective would free me from the burden and fear of these conflicts and unwanted consequences.

When confronted with conflicting perspectives, I am inclined to modify my belief system to avoid these conflicts instead of resolving them. When not grounded in eternal truth, the compromise that follows may drive me into the airy, foundationless nondescript.

> Out of the night that covers me,
> Black as the pit from pole to pole,
> I thank whatever gods may be
> For my unconquerable soul.
> In the fell clutch of circumstance
> I have not winced nor cried aloud.
> Under the bludgeonings of chance
> My head is bloody, but unbowed.
> Beyond this place of wrath and tears
> Looms but the Horror of the shade,
> And yet the menace of the years
> Finds and shall find me unafraid.
> It matters not how strait the gate,

How charged with punishments the scroll.
I am the master of my fate:
I am the captain of my soul.

-William Ernest Henley

Mr. Henley, defiant to his circumstances, stood proud to teach me a valuable lesson. I am the master of my fate and the captain of my soul. What is the meaning of this? It means that my perspective, my choices, my character, and ultimately my soul are guided and directed by my use of moral agency, independent of all earthly things. I may choose to be influenced but it is my prerogative, as a free agent thus designated by God, to incorporate these persuasions in my decision-making process, or not.

***

The law of opposition is the fundamental law that allows choice. My choices are what set me apart. They mold me and are molded by me. They benefit from a cause-and-effect relationship that makes it impossible to separate myself from my choices. I have the opportunity to act or to be acted upon.

Choice removes confusion and ambiguity and creates a state of being. Choice empowers, focuses, and imprints on my mind, body, and spirit. Choice builds integrity, crafts my character, strengthens determination, and ultimately defines me.

Through my choices, I become who I choose to become.

This is why the Lord's people are a covenant making and a covenant keeping people.

Worth

How do you know the worth of something?

By how much someone is willing to pay for it.

The following is a hypothetical situation loosely inspired by an actual event.

In 1933, a farmer from Springfield, Missouri, struck a rock while plowing his fields. The rock was moderately sized, though very heavy. Its position in the field was awkward and it was best if it was moved.

Being along in years, he was unable to move the rock on his own. He was left with two options, pay a local hand to help him get it into his truck and back to the barn, or plow around it. He opted to have it removed.

The farmer contacted Henry from the Oakstead farm, who promptly came out with his tractor to help him move the rock and only charged him $2 for the service.

Now that the rock was in his truck, he needed to figure out what to do with it. He brought it home and decided to clean it off to get a better look. It had a dark reddish hue to it, with pitting throughout and small angular holes, as if it had been a conglomerate that had lost some of its constituents.

His wife had a friend over who saw the rock in the back of the truck as the farmer was cleaning it off. She immediately took notice of it and thought it would look fabulous in her garden. She offered the farmer $20 if he would deliver it to her house.

Tempting as it was to make an $18 profit on this nuisance, the farmer declined. He took the rock to a friend of his who happened to be a bit of a rockhound and enjoyed this kind of thing.

His friend looked closer at the pitting and identified fractured olivine (peridot) imbedded within the rock and guessed that the rock was volcanic in nature, likely originating from deep within the earth. Fascinated by this find, the farmer's friend offered to buy the rock for $2000, as it would make a fine addition to his collection.

The farmer thanked his friend for his offer and his advice, and told him he would have to think about it.

The farmer continued to clean and examine his find. After removing the corrosion and excess left by centuries of exposure and neglect, he discovered that the rock was in fact a large piece of ore. He was not sure of what composition, though he assumed at least partially iron due to its weight and the reddish color of its initial appearance.

Ultimately, the farmer contacted a scientist, Henry Hamilton from Kansas, following a hunch. Mr. Hamilton confirmed his suspicion that the rock was not of this world. It was a meteorite.

Pieces of the Springfield meteorite eventually sold to a museum. It is estimated the museum paid over $650,000 for the 4.5 billion-year-old artifact.

***

At what point did that rock become valuable?

After it was cleaned, inspected, polished, cut, or appraised?

Did any of those activities change the fundamental characteristics of the rock and increase its value in any substantial way?

No! The properties of this rock that made it valuable were intrinsic to the rock itself and had existed within that rock ever since it came to this earth.

So it is with me, and all others who were born into this world. I have inherent worth in that I originate from heavenly parentage with divine purpose and potential. I have been bought with a price, infinite and eternal.

The Son of God offered Himself upon the alter to atone for my sins and transgressions. He gave all, that through His Grace I might overcome my weaknesses as I choose Him; as I choose life, agency, and joy. The Grace of Jesus Christ gives power to my righteous choices and covenants, and opens an effectual door that I may return to live with Him, and our Father, in the kingdom of God.

How do you know the worth of something?

By how much someone is willing to pay for it.

Jesus Christ descended below all things, that I might live, even life eternal with Him.

The Personal Nature of the Atonement

God the Father and His Son Jesus Christ are not as mortal men. They are not subject to the same limitations that we have placed upon ourselves. They are not subject to their physical bodies and senses; they command them and they have been adapted to their truest form.

If I allow myself to believe that the atonement of Jesus Christ was so large and took place over such a short period of time that it could not have possibly taken into account each individual, independent, personal suffering, struggle, trial and sin, I consign myself to be a member of the mass and all but overlooked in the grand scheme of eternal truths and purposes. This is untrue and a deplorable falsehood that is perpetuated by the adversary, the lover of lies.

The atonement of Jesus Christ was infinite and complete. He suffered individually for everyone. Through the Spirit of God, Jesus Christ was present during my suffering and suffered with me, for me. The atonement was performed while Jesus was in the world but not of the world.

Jesus Christ's sacrifice did not equate to the worst pain ever felt by mankind plus paying the price for the worst sin to be committed by mankind, thus being effectual for all other lesser pains and sins. I believe that Jesus affirms this in the book of Matthew.

> 37 Then shall the righteous answer him, saying, Lord, when saw we thee an hungred, and fed thee? or thirsty, and gave thee drink?

38 When saw we thee a stranger, and took thee in? or naked, and clothed thee?
39 Or when saw we thee sick, or in prison, and came unto thee?
40 And the King shall answer and say unto them, Verily I say unto you, Inasmuch as ye have done it unto one of the least of these my brethren, ye have done it unto me.

Matthew 25:37-39 (KJV)

Jesus declared that when I serve one of the least of these, His brethren, I have done it unto Him.

How is that possible?

Why is that possible?

When I remove suffering from the world, I remove suffering from the burden of Christ. As the Lord and Savior of mankind moved through the ages in experiencing the pains and sufferings of His people, our acts of kindness, alleviating suffering from this life, ultimately eliminate it from the Savior's mission.

Likewise, when suffering is inflicted or allowed to endure, the suffering of the Savior is condoned, and He is offered up on the altar of His sacrifice on behalf of those persons.

God is Love

So, what is Love?

Some might argue that if you knew everything there was to know about a person, you could anticipate their responses to any given situation. This argument is extended to explain the omniscience of the Almighty in that He can "read the source code" and can therefore "anticipate the outcome." God's omniscience comes from knowing, not anticipating.

God broke the "source code" the moment He perfected it, when He endowed us with moral agency. Moral agency dictates that in spite of all or none of our experiences, environmental factors, preconceived notions, predispositions, whatever, I have the opportunity, ability, and responsibility to choose for myself. I may act or allow myself to be acted upon.

The gift of moral agency is a crowning attribute of mankind.

God has not forsaken me; He is giving me the opportunity to grow and to own what can truly be owned. He is ever mindful of me and my situation and loves me with a perfect love. As such, He perceives the eternal consequences of action or inaction and directs His attentions toward that of eternal worth.

Moral agency is the most intimate, personal aspect of my existence, and the only facet of my life over which I have complete control, and for which I hold sole accountability. I believe it is requisite with the justice of God that mankind has the opportunity to exercise their moral agency in the definition of their individual character.

This existence is and always has been built upon the exalting principle of moral agency.

As a man thinketh in his heart, so is he. Prov. 23:7 (KJV)

My world is shaped by how I perceive it.

The actuality or existence of times and events, independent of my direct influence, are not molded or altered because I will it to be so. It is altered by how I choose to perceive and relate to it. Accepting or rejecting truth does not alter truth.

God is love.

When I stand before God in a resurrected perfected state, if I have received Him, I will see as I am seen, and know as I am known, having received of his fullness and of his Grace. If I am faithful I will see God in my eternal state, and through the Grace of Jesus Christ I will be like Him.

God views me as I truly am and as I may become. Can I see as I am seen now? Can we see others as they are seen now?

I believe that seeing through the eyes of God is to "know" God, to "receive" God, to know the love of God!

The Lord has commanded us to be one, for if we are not one, we are not His. How do we become one? I believe we become one as we unite ourselves through the will and Spirit of God, take up our cross, and yoke ourselves with Christ. Jesus Christ *"took upon Himself every pain, every sin, and all of the anguish and suffering ever experienced by you and me and by everyone who has ever lived or will ever live."* (Russell M. Nelson, The Correct Name of the Church Oct. 2018)

The atonement is not an impersonal event that occurred thousands of years ago. The power, reach, and influence of Jesus Christ's condescension continue today. In His suffering and through His Grace, Jesus reaches into the eternities and touches every life, in every moment, as He bares our suffering with us.

God is love. This eternal love can be had in and through Jesus Christ and His atonement. My love for Christ and my unanswerable debt to Him have bound me to Him.

This bond in turn binds me to others, for Christ has suffered for all, the just and the unjust. My love for Christ and my sorrow at His suffering turn my heart to Him, and through Him my heart is turned to my neighbor.

When I yoke myself with Christ, when I mourn with those who mourn, comfort those who stand in need of comfort, when I become a peacemaker, when I bear others' burdens, and seek to do and inspire good, I make a choice.

I am enabled to become my best self as I choose Grace and follow the path of my great Exemplar, even Jesus Christ.

Becoming

There are many different and diverse approaches to becoming. I struggle with defining what becoming means to me. As my life progresses, what shape do I want it to take and how can I assist in the realization of its reality?

What do I want to do?

What brings me joy?

Exploring these questions leads me to contemplate various vocations, hobbies, or interests. Some bring temporary fun or excitement. Others leave a more lasting influence, though perspective and pursuit are lacking.

For example, attending college and leaving with a degree was a rewarding, yet challenging, endeavor. Confident this was a worthy, admirable goal and activity, I tackled it without question.

While gaining an education and expanding my mind was part of my becoming, going to college was not.

Where was the disconnect?

How might I hinder my progress with a pit stop at college?

It wasn't college. It was my perspective of college. I needed more. College came and college went.

My becoming is not a series of events or activities to be participated in. My becoming is integral and ingrained. It is perpetual.

What did I want to be?

I want to be successful, useful, and valued. I sought a career where I could utilize my love for science, mathematics, and nature. Exploring multiple options, I bounced between several majors, drifting more and more technical as my understanding and aptitude for mathematics increased, ultimately settling on geological sciences.

Was I a scientist, a geologist, or a geophysicist?

Did I find success and utility?

Did I offer value to the world?

What was I becoming?

Again, this perspective left me wanting.

It wasn't what I was that gave me fulfillment. Title, money, or recognition did not bring joy, nor did they give any lasting satisfaction. They are fleeting. They must be continually guarded and sought after. Ever leading, never finding.

***

How do I find purpose and meaning?

Where does my journey begin?

Who do I want to become?

What is happiness and where do I find it?

Happiness is found in joy, fulfillment, and peace. Happiness is found when I stand independent and confident in any circumstance. Happiness is found when I embrace faith, love, and hope outside of and in spite of my fear. Happiness is found as I become more like my Savior, Jesus Christ, through the enabling power of his atonement.

***

The atonement of Jesus Christ is a free gift, offered to all. Like the light of the sun, the Son of God has performed His great work on our behalf, and the love, light, and power of that work fills the immensity of space. The influence of the Lord's sacrifice can be accessed by all who desire to do so.

As with the light of the sun, certain aspects of the atonement are effectual universally. The light of the sun influences times, seasons, temperature, and weather patterns, among other notable aspects of our lives.

Everyone who has been or ever will be born into mortality will die. We have not been given power or choice over this inevitability. As such, through Jesus Christ we will overcome this obstacle. Resurrection is a free gift to all who are subject to mortal life and death.

Other aspects of the sun, though given without money or price, require our commitment and action. If we wish to benefit from the light and rays of the sun, we must step out of the shadows. Solar panels, flowers, algae, and many other plants and animals require direct sunlight to thrive, flourish, and grow.

Their need to "step" into the light does not change the nature of the sun's light, nor does it impose any cost or requirements stipulated by the sun. It is inherent in the light that we must position ourselves in the path of the light's influence.

So it is with the atonement of Jesus Christ. If we seek to be cleansed, enabled, buoyed, strengthened, or empowered by Christ and His atonement, we must position ourselves in the path of the light's influence.

How do I step into the light?

What must I do to shed the dark night of despair and wanting?

I need only choose Grace, come unto Christ, and become. Choosing Grace is choosing Jesus Christ and His atonement.

These choices are not made frivolously. I should approach the God of Life intentionally, with integrity. I unlock the power of the Lord's atonement as I perform covenants with Him, in his name and in His way. He has prescribed means and methods for stepping out of the darkness and into the light. As I covenant with Him, He seals my choice with divine power and promise.

The marriage and sealing ordinance is the crowning covenant our Father offers us in this life. Joining in holy matrimony with a bond and covenant, binding beyond this life and into the eternities, is the most holy act in our mortal becoming. I am to step out of my selfish, independent self and become greater, joined with another.

We become as our Heavenly Parentage and share in their glory. They have gifted Their power and privilege to us as we share in the creation of life and nurture our family. As children are born within this sacred covenant of marriage, the binding power extends and propagates. This propagation continues forward, backward, and sideways, as long and as far as we are able and willing to enter into these covenants with our God.

**

Jesus Christ is a perfect gentleman. It is not His will to impose Himself on anyone. He seeks to make Himself known, then allows us the opportunity to accept His love and hope or to remain in the shadows of fear, doubt, and despair.

I progress toward Christ through the gift of Holy Ghost, empowered and enabled through the Grace of Jesus Christ's atonement as I make and honor my covenants. As I acknowledge my faults and weaknesses and give them to the Savior, He transforms my weaknesses into strengths. In my weakness, yoked with and empowered by Christ, my fear turns to courageous love, doubt transforms into abiding faith, and despair blossoms into divine hope.

The ultimate purpose of the atonement of Jesus Christ is not to just cleanse us from our sins. It is to facilitate, enable, and empower our greatest becoming.

Other Writings

Equality

Entering in silence,
into thy holy presence,
to kneel in reverence
at thy Throne.
Repentance committed,
forgiveness is granted,
as hailing angels
welcome home.

Keys and Stones,
Books and Thrones,
are gifts the Lord has stored.
A simple man,
who follows a dream,
let peace be my reward.

Faith vs Fear

A little deeper,
please don't waiver.
It's your conviction,
now feel my pain.

Hurting my heart,
to fill a heart of your own.
I understand your possession,
now understand mine,
and be freed.

Awaken

When you can't witness
His subtleties and grace,
credit is due to the one
who runs the impious race.
Unite the internal divide;
abolish the conflict that dies.
Remember He always Loves you;
there is never a reason to hide.

He comforts me with the
children's smiles,
hides amidst a poet's rain.
I see Him from a mountain's
peak,
a force I will never tame.
He will tell me a secret,
Beauty my Heart must see.
In good time,
He will sing me a song.
He lives in the future for me.

Love Is the Key

Darkness chills, the pale heart
fills
with love's grown anguish
cries.
A rose in thorns, as beauty forms
the season takes;

it dies.

Midday's moon, was wand'ring
through
the depth of nights now gone.
A face once formed, inside the
storm
awakened to the dawn.
Overwhelmed, the sight in view
shows beauty, sweet medley.

Then through the day,
this song is heard
"I know that love's the key."

Light departs, her eyes turn east
awaiting love's return.

Morning breaks,

a whisper speaks
"We are here to love and learn."

Potential

Hands with power, unseen vision,
understand yourself and you'll go
further.
Lift your head and stand tall.
He can see you, why can't you?
Stop and look into your past
Who was that?
Look into the mirror; who is that?
Look through the eyes of our
Father.
Who can you be?

Unexplored potential,
sands of the hour glass.
Exploring your potential reveals

–divine substance–
to the inevitable laps called
– change –

Break the barrier and push
yourself;
reach for the unreachable.
He will make up the rest,
for we are the children of the
Most
High
God.

Reveal

Then I heard the thunder rap and
roar,
lightning flashed,
striking to the core. and
Even though I felt it no one
heard.
It
carried on the wind
and then I burned it.

Breaking through the glass I
found myself
stared at by the Lord,
ashamed of myself.
He opened up my eyes so I could
see
all the horror and the pain.
Oh! It's me!

I need to find peace,
I can't stand it.
"Come follow me; consider it
granted."

He broke the ugly mold and
made a new one.
He told me a secret
and called me His son.

Love is the secret and He wants it
done.
Show the whole world that they
may be
ONE!

Satan's Fog

Haunting 'til dusk,
hunting 'til dawn,

escape and retreat,
only delays a fight.

Cursing my existence,
brings my sorrow forth.

Understanding the Word,
would determine the Truth,
hence putting my grief to rest.

Angels Have Told

Angels have told
from days of old
Of Jesus Lord and King.
A virgin birth
would bless the earth,
then righteous men
would sing.

O, glory to the Lord of Lords,
who stands and reigns on high.
We love the word that feeds our
souls;
His voice shall never die.

A newfound life
In a love for Christ,
Our heavenly souls rejoice.
And with the love
and gospel's song,
We are also given choice.

Now it came pass
to confirm the word
A babe was born of God.
A gift of love
To all the earth,
for he carries the iron rod.

A rod that leads unto the tree
whose fruit is for mankind.
A love from God
to bless the sick,
and give sight unto the blind.

Blessed is he,
the one who sees
the light but has no eyes.
His faith is strong,
His sight will come,
For Jesus hears his cries.

O, Glory to the King of Kings
who stands and reigns on high.
We love the word
That feeds our souls;
His voice shall never die

Jesus bleeds
For you and me
On the cross at Calvary.
He is put away
for three long days
then rose unto Mary.

Journey

Walking through a mist of
questions,
No answers.

Finding a way with an
outstretched hand
and a foot on the floor.

Groping through the mist of
obscurity,
wandering in a darkness
under the heat of a Sun.
At noon,
full grandeur atop the world.

Absorbed into the shadow of
feeling,
never looking up.

Study the impression of a
silhouette as it flows,
flowing over the undulations of
the passing ground.

Cerebral silence;
silence so thick you can hear the
movement of the blood in your
veins.
Where thoughts come so loudly
they penetrate your
consciousness
with a dominance that owns all
other senses.

A sound;
Not a breath, a blink or a
swallow.
Look up only to be blinded;
Blinded by the light,
only the absence of which has
created the negative so
captivating.

Retiring back to the comfort of
the abyss,
the familiarity of shadow.

Temporary solace in the
simplicity that is me.
My understanding
the idle thoughts of pleasure and
survival.

Continually the light and the
wonder that is offered
returns to the mind.
The eye is drawn to conclude
that it is the source of all
understanding.
Without the light
Shadow is only a thought;
Darkness leans to the light to
exist.

Squinting your eyes
you strive to face the light,
The warmth of the Sun.
Discomfort and pain accompany
the first impressions.
Yet the curiosity
the hope that the light affords—
A greater perspective;

Strengthen the will and harden
the resolve;
push forward and acclimate.

Dilation permits the progression
of absorption.
It becomes apparent that life in
the shadow
was no life at all.

Confined in the middle of the
potential of life,
yet even with full view of the
surrounding landscape,
all that the light seems to be
touching.

The field is limited.
Observing the path of the
shadow's journey
the horizon swallows the option
for seeing beyond recent
memory.

Journey's origin,
unknown,
captivating.

As sailors from days long ago,
the trail is eaten by absence and
void,
suggesting extinction before
existence.

The mind's eye
blurred.
The spirit knows more.

Made in the USA
Lexington, KY
22 September 2019